Raising Success

How to Give Your Child an Academic Edge

It's Easier Than You Think!

By Grace Sullivan

NOTICE
WARNING CONCERNING COPYRIGHT RESTRICTIONS

The copyright law of the United States [Title 17, United States Code] governs the making of photocopies or other reproductions of copyrighted material.

Under certain conditions specified in the law, libraries and archives are authorized to furnish a photocopy or other reproduction. One of these specific conditions is that the photocopy or reproduction is not to be "used for any purpose other than private study, scholarship, or research." If a user makes a request for, or later uses, a photocopy or reproduction for purposes in excess of "fair use," that user may be liable for copyright infringement.

This institution reserves the right to refuse to accept a copying order if, in its judgment, fulfillment of the order would involve violation of copyright law. No further reproduction and distribution of this copy is permitted by transmission or any other means.

Table of Contents

PRESCHOOL YEARS 10

ELEMENTARY SCHOOL YEARS 16

MIDDLE SCHOOL YEARS 22

HIGH SCHOOL YEARS 30

MATH REVIEW FOR THE SAT EXAM 48

ADVICE ON THE ESSAY FOR THE SAT EXAM 126

400 VOCABULARY WORDS FOR THE SSAT 148

Preface

I DIDN'T WANT to write this book... At least, not at first.

***

I GREW UP in a large family with five brothers and sisters. I always remember my parents being very relaxed, and I think that's because they were living in the eye of the storm, with the six of us kids as the surrounding hurricane. Being in such a large family, individual attention was hard to come by. You had to learn to speak up, and if you wanted something you were going to have to go about getting it yourself. My parents didn't have time to proof read my essays or make sure I practiced my sport or my musical instrument. They certainly loved me, but they had enough on their plate with five other kids to worry about whether or not I had handed in my science project on time. So I scraped by. I was pretty smart and did pretty well, but I didn't stand out.

Fast forward: I'm holding my first baby for the very first time, a beautiful girl named Holly. At that moment, I love that baby more than anything else in the world. As they say, there's nothing like a mother's love. Right there, looking into her eyes, I think of a decision I made long ago, back in my childhood when if I wasn't quick enough to the lunch table, my sandwich would be gone: I promised myself that I was going to make sure Holly got all the love and attention she deserved. I was going to do everything I could to help her succeed and live a happy, carefree life. Holly would never have to wonder how she could have fared if only she had her mother's focus and attention upon her.

An important distinction to note in this era of "Tiger moms" and overbearing parents: I was not deciding to *make* my daughter succeed, but to *allow* her to flourish. Out of love, not ambition, was I going to look out for her, give her the best, and help her to be the best that Holly could be. I heaved no standards or expectations upon her. My definition of "success" was not an Ivy League admissions letter. It was not an SAT score, nor a GPA, nor an MVP award. It was important to me that we remained who we were – getting an A on a test was not worth sacrificing a happy home and a happy daughter. I used to encourage my daughter to read, not so that she would score better on reading comprehension exams, but so that she might develop a life-long love of reading. Whether Holly was learning phonics as a little girl or studying for the SAT as a high schooler, I always allowed her to take a break if the task became too overwhelming. Indeed, all I wanted for my daughter was for her to be happy and to be the best "Holly" that she could be. To me, as a mother, that would be true success.

***

WHICH BRINGS ME to why I didn't initially want to write this book.

Through a combination of good fortune, intuition, and guidance, Holly developed into a wonderful young girl. She got good grades, stood out on various athletic fields, and developed a strong sense of confidence. Most of all, she was happy and relaxed. Busy, but not overwhelmed, Holly excelled while leading an uncluttered, authentic life.

Many other parents thought that Holly got good grades just because she was "naturally smart," but that in order for their children to really excel in school, they would have to turn into overbearing figures, "tiger" or "helicopter" moms or dads, watching their kids like hawks and driving them like slaves until they achieved certain goals or marks. They thought they would have to instill strict discipline and drive out fun. This is a risky recipe for academic results, one that could just as easily result in epic failure as success, and one that would certainly lead to an unhappy lifestyle at the very least.

With this common misperception being generally accepted as the way things had to be, it was here that I found parents typically divided into two camps. On the one hand, some parents thought that all this sounded like a nightmare, and that no matter what kind of grades their kids would achieve, the ends wouldn't justify the means. These parents wanted an authentic life; to them, academic success just wasn't worth adopting these measures and pushing their kids to be something they weren't. As a cop out, these parents often would say things like, "Well, many CEO's were C students, you know…" Besides the obvious fact that students who excel in school *usually* go to better colleges and have better jobs, the underlying implication here is what really scared me. Are we to settle for mediocrity and allow kids to scrape by (like I did) when they are capable of something more? I could not accept that.

On the other hand, some parents felt that the ends definitely justified the means. To these parents, admission into a top prep school, or later, to an elite university, justified any means necessary. These parents bought every review book and "insider" tale out there, and they often spent thousands of dollars on tutoring and prep courses. Seeing Holly's success, these were the parents who first approached me about writing a book. They wanted to know how my child got good grades, and how I raised a child that got A's and got accepted into every Ivy League school without spending a dime on prep courses or tutoring. To them, all this made Holly a success. But when I looked at Holly, I saw a happy, confident girl who was being the best that she could be. I saw a successful girl who got good grades, not a girl who was successful *because* she got good grades.

***

Ironically, it was my disagreements with both of these parenting camps that led me to write this book. First of all, I disagreed with the very principle that becoming a "tiger" mom was necessary for academic success. In fact, my views didn't align with either side: I thought that becoming a "tiger" mom *did* sound like a nightmare, but I also knew that **stress-free ways of helping your child** *did* exist. I knew that you didn't have to push a child to be something she's not in order to achieve success. It's all about putting them in position to excel. Indeed, there are simple, proven techniques, there are key decisions to be made, and there are pitfalls to avoid – in short, there is a definitely a "smart" way to navigate a child's academic path and achieve the fulfillment of potential. And it doesn't take sacrificing your relationships to get there.

My passion in life is seeing **the fulfillment of potential**, and conversely, my greatest frustration is seeing a child's potential go unfulfilled. This passion, coupled with a mother's love for her daughter, is what enabled Holly to be the best "Holly" she could be. She was pretty smart, but I knew Holly didn't excel simply on smarts alone. No one does. Whether they realize it or not, everyone who excels in anything owes at least some of their success to outside forces. We are a product of our environment. I put Holly in a position to have an edge, to develop self-confidence, and to have the message, "I'm smart!" be reinforced over and over again. The decisions I made and methods I used put Holly in a position to get the best grades she possibly could while still maintaining a happy, authentic lifestyle.

As I gained experience through being a mother, through teaching and tutoring for twenty years, through studying at one Ivy League University's graduate school of education, and through chatting up people of all backgrounds and levels of expertise, hearing their stories of what worked and what didn't, I began to realize that the steps I had taken with Holly – when and how to study or prepare, how to make sure she always had an edge at every step of the journey – were less specific and more universal than I had ever imagined. As I started to realize that most students were actually capable of getting A's and doing well on standardized exams, my passion for seeing potential fulfilled ignited and flared.

It was because of this passion that I started sharing my experiences, my tips, my advice to all those who were calling me for council on academic matters. I was consulting for parents with children of all ages, fielding questions ranging from what kindergarten to attend to getting an edge on the SAT's, to giving high schoolers their best shot in the college admissions process. I couldn't stand seeing a child go through life thinking that they did poorly academically because they "didn't test well" or were just "dumb." I believe that such a child just wasn't put in position to succeed.

As my reputation for possessing keen insight and giving sound advice began to grow (to the point where complete strangers were contacting me!) I began to think about heeding the cries of many and sharing my knowledge in a book. It was a vast undertaking, to say the least. I had all my personal experiences to cover. I had the detailed blueprint that I followed with Holly (the books I used, the study methods I taught her, the schedules and timetables I followed, the decisions I made), from her time in preschool, elementary and middle school, through high school and, finally, through the college applications and Ivy League admissions processes.

I had the experiences of all my friends and Holly's friends, stories of how other students played it right, and the stories of the many who unfortunately played it wrong. Indeed, I know many - too many - parents who made poor, uninformed decisions for their bright, high-achieving children that came back to haunt them during the college admissions process. (Don't worry, all of these horror stories are included for your benefit – learn from their mistakes!)

I also had the experiences gained through twenty years of teaching at some of the best private schools in the country while also observing some of the best – and worst – public schools. I had the experiences from tutoring hundreds of students from public, private, and home schools alike, which has given me some of my proudest moments as I have helped them achieve tremendous success in advising them on their academic paths and on college applications. I also had my experiences and knowledge gained through studying at one Ivy League university's graduate school of education, where I completed a research project on the finer points of achieving success on the math sections of the SAT exam. I had all this and more, and I've included it all in *Raising Success*. I've changed some names out of respect for privacy (my daughter is not actually named Holly), but other than that, I haven't held anything back. It's all here for your benefit, and I guarantee you'll pick up at least one pearl of wisdom along the way.

***

I HAVE ALWAYS admired the book *What to Expect When You're Expecting*. With over 14.5 million copies in print, it's a book that almost every pregnant woman reads. It is virtually required reading for a pregnant woman. The book has all the advice, tips, and facts – everything you need to know for every step of the journey – all in one place. I have read almost every book out there on parenting, raising academically successful kids, and getting into college, and I believe that the parenting world is lacking a *What to Expect* kind of book. For some reason, you can get all the advice and knowledge you need up until the moment your child is born, but from then on you're on your own. For the most part, you're wading through an overwhelming mass of information and misinformation, an unorganized jumble of conflicting theories and clichés. I have set out to put an end to this noise and to assemble everything you need to know all in one place. It has indeed been a massive undertaking, but it's been a burden of love. *Raising Success* is a lifetime's worth of experiences, a comprehensive roadmap for every step from preschool to college. By the final page, you will know exactly what to expect. You will have all the experience and wisdom of this seasoned mother, and be able to **approach every step with the clear perspective of hindsight.** Most of all, you will be able to put your child in a position to be the best that he or she can possibly be. You will be able to raise a *true* success.

Preschool Years

Preschool Years

Socializing is one of the most important aspects of your child's development during the preschool years. I chose a local preschool that was not academic at all. I felt it was most important for my child to love school and not have anyone make her feel embarrassed or inadequate because she didn't know something.

No matter how smart you believe your child is, do not push her ahead. Even if she knows her numbers and letters before the start of the 3 year-old class, let her stay in that class and become a leader. Let her work on her social skills in school. You can supplement your child academically at home with workbooks and educational computer games.

My oldest daughter had a November birthday, so she started the 3-year old class in September and turned 4 in November. Being one of the oldest, her experience from her first day of school was a very positive, confident one. She knew her letters and numbers at 3 ¾ years old, and so she always felt like she knew the answers to teacher's questions. More importantly, she had fun, and loved school.

I felt it was most important that my daughter feel confident and get used to the idea, 'Hey, I'm smart!' I didn't want her going to an overly aggressive academic preschool where she might not know the answer to some questions and get discouraged or become disengaged.

In contrast, a friend of mine sent her daughter to a more rigorous, academic preschool that made her daughter feel embarrassed for not knowing her address and phone number when she was only 3 years old.

Another friend pushed her daughter who had an October birthday ahead into the 4 year-old class because she was very advanced academically. She was a very bright girl, but she never developed great social skills. Four year-olds are often not interested in socializing with someone younger, especially someone who knows more answers than they do. This child would have been much better off in the 3 year-old class with other kids her age and supplemented academically at home. This is a great example of why socializing should be a huge priority in the early years.

Some preschool teachers will tell you your child doesn't need to know any letters or numbers before kindergarten. I promise you that some students will be arriving on the first day of kindergarten fully reading books on their own.

In order for your child to feel confident academically, I feel it's very important for her to know the alphabet, the numbers through 10, and the phonic sounds for basic 3 letter words. Since they go over this during kindergarten, if your child already has a strong base, the message of "you're smart" will be delivered over and over again to your child. The feeling of comfort they will gain during classroom discussions will increase their confidence.

I also went to a local Walmart store and bought a few **preschool workbooks that reviewed the alphabet and numbers.** I would go over the easy pages with my daughter only when it was convenient and we were both in the mood. I bought the workbook "**An I know it! Book,**" published by **School Zone Publishing Company**.

When she knew her letters, I bought a **preschool workbook on phonics**. Again, I would go over the pages with her when we were both in the mood to do so. The key is to never push too hard. Always stop when either of you has had enough. Instilling a love for reading during these early years can prove invaluable over time. The more books you can read to your child on a nightly basis, the better.

So, before my daughter started Kindergarten she knew all her numbers and letters and had a good idea about the basic phonic sounds. **Leap Frog** makes a great phonics game where you put a card into a small travel sized machine, and you can press the letters to hear the sound. The child sees a picture of a car and the letters car. When they press the letters, they hear the sound the letters make.

It is not necessary to become a teacher or buy the intense $300 phonics game systems (although they are good). A simple phonics game, either travel size or a computer game, is plenty for your child to be introduced to phonics and get the idea about sounds. Moreover, simple, easy workbooks from any Walmart or drug store will also do nicely.

If you are applying your child to a private school kindergarten, he or she definitely needs to know numbers, letters, and basic phonic sounds. Children usually are asked to draw a picture of themselves because the more detailed the picture is, the more intelligent they are believed to be. Have your child practice drawing pictures of people and remind them to include eyebrows, ears, eyelashes, hands, feet, a pocketbook, earrings, and etc.

At the private schools in our area, a child will be asked if he/she knows letters, numbers, to read a few easy words, and to draw a picture of themselves. They need to be able to shake the Admissions person's hand and look in them in the eye when they say, "Hello."

If you are very interested in sending your child to a private school, sometimes bribery works well! Have a present wrapped in the car that the child knows he gets after he shakes hands and has his best manners during the interview. I also never told my kids it was an interview. In order to take away any pressure, I told them that they were just going to visit the schools to see which they liked better.

Make sure your child is well rested during the Admissions interview. I know a mom who had her son signed up for so many activities that he arrived at the Kindergarten interview exhausted and unprepared. He was a great kid, but he did not get in to that school. He was too tired to be polite and answer questions well.

***

I know of one mom who was told that anything academic during preschool was unnecessary, as her son would learn everything in kindergarten. Well, her son arrived in kindergarten knowing nothing while a large group of children already knew their letters and numbers, and many other kids were even reading on their own. Her son was a shy child, and not knowing any letters, numbers, or phonic sounds only made him doubt himself and retreat into himself even more. He understandably felt uncomfortable and thought he wasn't as smart as his peers. Now going into 3rd grade, he's just starting to come out of his shell, and his confidence level is still relatively low.

Imagine if his mother had helped him learn his letters, numbers, and simple phonetic sounds before he went to kindergarten. He would have sat in that classroom and known the answers, felt smart, and would been told, "You're right" so many times that his confidence would have soared.

This mother's attitude was that any child reading in kindergarten was like a monkey who was taught to read in that neither the child nor the monkey would really understand the content of what they were reading. She may have had a point, but kindergarteners that know how to read even at a basic level from the get-go know are going to feel more confident. They'll know and understand everything that is being discussed in class. They won't feel lost: the message, "you're smart," is reinforced to them every day. Compare that to the child who sits there not knowing his letters or numbers or any phonics as he watches the other kids know what they're doing. No wonder he was shy and scared and felt alienated him from the class.

***

Conclusion

- Keep **socializing** a major priority during the preschool years.
- Make sure your child knows the **alphabet, numbers 1 through 10, and beginner phonetic sounds for common, easy 3-letter words before they go to kindergarten.**
- **Read** as often as you can to them and/or have babysitters read to them.
- If your child is close to the cut-off date for preschool, now is your chance to hold him/her back! Once you start a school in kindergarten, it becomes very difficult to hold a child back. **Public schools simply do not allow you to hold your child back unless he/she completely flunks kindergarten.** If you chose a private school, who wants to hold a child back and pay for kindergarten twice?
- In general, the older your child is in the grade, the better they will do! **Maturity and confidence have everything to do with learning!**
- I have yet to meet a parent who has not regretted putting their child in the situation of being the youngest in their class! Even if your child is academically ready, they will most likely suffer socially down the road. The decision of when to send your child to school demands consideration on the impact the timing will have on their learning, social life, and experience in sports. Giving your child every advantage you can starts with preschool!
- **You don't have to become a teacher**. Get a simple workbook and have your kids do a page a day, perhaps 5 out of 7 days a week. They can do it at the table while you make dinner, for example, and if they have a question, they can ask you. Make it easy and fun, never overwhelming or too rigorous. One page a day is plenty. If you're busy, have them do it with a babysitter, or if possible ask the daycare to help them do it.
- Educational computer games that teach letters, numbers, and phonic sounds are also great, and they do not require you to be too involved.
- **Rewards are great to motivate children**. "If you do a page, you can watch a TV show" (or get something else they want). When they finish the book, they get a reward.
  - My younger son will do anything to watch a TV show, so I sometimes bribe him by telling him he has to do some work in his book in order to be able to watch his favorite show. It's amazing how eager he is to do the work knowing he gets what he wants when he's done!

Elementary School Years

ELEMENTARY SCHOOL YEARS
(Grades 1-5)

During the elementary school years, **mastering the basics** is the most important goal. It's all right not to be a straight A student at this point, as long as the child is learning from his mistakes.

Private or public school can be equally good, as long as the basics are being mastered. **The secret to this is the summer!**

Every summer, go to a bookstore and get a summer workbook for the grade level your child just completed. The child should do one page a day, 5 out of 7 days a week, along with reading some books. A very academically advanced private school near me has their students completing a **Summer Skills workbook** for math. These Summer Skills Workbooks review everything that was taught that previous year. By having your child review the concepts over the summer, they cement their skills and fill in any areas they forgot or didn't understand initially, so he or she enters the next grade with a solid foundation. You can order these books at www.summerskills.com. There are 30 lessons, so have them complete 10 in June, 10 in July, and 10 in August.

They also have a **Language Arts workbook**. If your child can do both the math and language arts books every summer **for the grade level she just completed**, she will be building a very strong foundation for the next year.

The critical point to remember, however, is that the learning takes place in the corrections. It's no good to do the work in the workbooks if the children are not learning from their mistakes. The pages have to be corrected and reviewed with the child in order for your child to improve his or her knowledge.

After first grade and second grade, your kids should master their addition and subtraction problems. A book called **The Mad Minute (Mastering Number Facts Grades 1–8)** is a fantastic tool, and can be ordered online. Children should practice a few pages a day during the summer, or on weekends during the school year. **These Mad Minute** books are great because they give a page of random addition problems that can be photo copied for extra practice. The method of doing sequential problems, (20 + 1, 20 + 2, 20 + 3, etc), is not as good because kids can often pick up the pattern, in which case they are not actually solving the problem. Kumon worksheets are sequential, and therefore, I never paid for a Kumon class or bought any of their workbooks. **Mad Minutes** should be done along with the **Summer Skills** workbooks.

How fast the child completes the practice math sheets at home during the summer is NOT important. If your child does 3 **Mad Minute** sheets over breakfast, 5 out of 7 days a week, he or she will naturally increase their speed by the end of the summer. Repetition will develop speed and accuracy.

I made 3 copies by each page so that my child had to do the same page, with the same problems, while eating her breakfast. For children who love to watch cartoons on TV, tell them they can watch them after they finish 3 sheets, and you will be amazed at how quickly they will be done. But make sure they don't just copy a sheet they already completed!

Flash cards have never worked for us, and they require a lot of parent-involved time. Worksheets, on the other hand, are great because the child can do them on their own while breakfast or dinner is being made.

Remember, learning takes place in the corrections!

***

Conclusion

- During the elementary school years, get a **<u>Summer Skills</u>** workbook and the **<u>Mad Minute</u>** workbook, and have your child do one page a day as often as possible during the summer. The **<u>Mad Minutes</u>** worksheets help them to master their facts, while the **<u>Summer Skills</u>** worksheets review the concepts they need to understand. Also, try to have a regular reading time each night before bedtime. Children are often willing to read anything if it means they get to stay up an extra 20 minutes.

- **<u>Summertime is the secret</u>!** Your kids don't need tutors or summer school. They can still go to camp or do sports or travel on a family vacation. Just have them do a page or two over breakfast, and then they'll have the rest of the day to play. After a whole summer of reinforcing the skills they've learned, you'll be surprised at how ready they are for school in September.
    - **Summer between first and second grade: master the addition facts.**
    - **Summer between second and third grade: master addition and subtraction facts.**
    - **Summer between third and fourth grade: master the multiplication and division facts.**
    - (This can be altered by a year)

- Studies have shown that students who know their addition, subtraction, multiplication, and division facts **<u>before</u>** entering middle school do **<u>much</u>** better in middle school math. By the end of the 4th or 5th grade, if your child has mastered these facts, has practiced the Language Arts Summer Skills workbook every summer, and has read as much as possible, he or she will be in a great position entering middle school.

- If your school starts standardized testing in 3rd grade, you should buy any book that has practice exams or problems for that exam and have your child do as much as possible during the summer before entering the grade in which they will be tested. **Practice questions and learning from mistakes are the keys to acing standardized exams! Practice exams have to be corrected and the mistakes reviewed with the student in a helpful, constructive (not punitive) way.**

    If you cannot find a practice book for the exact standardized exam your child will take, any standardized exam practice book for that grade level should be sufficient.

Middle School Years

Middle School Years

If your child has a choice of languages to study, I would **absolutely insist they take Latin!** If they don't have the ability to take Latin in Middle School, start freshman year in high school. **<u>Insist on Latin</u>**. Studying Latin provides huge advantages on board exams in high school, as Latin students who don't know a word on the test can figure out its meaning from its roots, and Latin is very helpful in understanding parts of speech. Moreover, if your child chooses to study another language after learning Latin, they will be able to pick it up more easily.

I know two very intelligent students who had difficulty scoring well on the reading comprehension section of the SAT because of the vocabulary in the readings. They both had gone to public school through eighth grade and then to one of the top academic private boarding schools in the country. Their math skills were great, but even despite the very strong English department in their high school, they both struggled to understand the meanings of some of the readings on the SAT reading comprehension section due to the vocabulary in the readings. Their vocabulary held them back. They both had studied Spanish in high school, and had they chosen Latin, I assure you their reading score would have been higher.

I told my daughter that once she learned Latin, she could take any language she wanted to in college. She is currently taking Spanish as a freshman, absolutely loving the class and picking up the language very easily. She credits her high school Latin for her success on her reading comprehension board scores, which helped her get accepted by multiple Ivy League colleges.

***

Make sure your kids have **completed Algebra 1 by the end of eighth grade**. Studies have shown that students who have *not* completed Algebra 1 by the end of eighth grade score much lower on standardized exams in high school.

The SAT and the ACT exams both cover math through the level of Algebra 2. **Your kids need to have <u>completed Algebra 2 by the end of sophomore year</u> so they can prepare for the SAT during that summer.**

If you cannot get your children to complete Algebra 1 by the end of eighth grade, another option would be to have them take a summer course to get them on a schedule that has them completing Algebra 1, Geometry, and Algebra 2 by the end of sophomore year. Other options, especially if your child is young for her grade, would be to have her repeat 8th grade, or start 9th grade in one high school and then transfer to another and repeat 9th grade.

***

The SSAT Exam

The SSAT is an exam for entrance into a private high school. (It is different than the SAT.)

During the summers after 6th grade, buy an SSAT study guide and have your kids take multiple practice exams, even if you're sending your child to a public high school. Taking these practice exams will help your child build and cement a foundation they will need not only to excel in high school, but also to excel on the board exam they will take to apply to college. **Remember, practice questions and learning from mistakes are the keys to excelling on standardized exams!**

www.ssat.org, the website of the maker of the exam, provides a study guide that is typically slightly easier than the actual exam, and is a good place to start. **Princeton Review** has a study guide that is closest to the level of the actual exam. Barron's is usually the most difficult, so once your child has completed all the practice exams from the SSAT study guide, and then the **Princeton Review,** it's a good time to try the ones in **Barron's**.

The SSAT exam has 4 sections: reading comprehension, two math sections, and vocabulary with analogies. Have your child spend no more than an hour a day on trying to complete as much as they can in that hour. **It is NOT important to time them!** If they complete all the practice sections on 8 exams, they will become extremely proficient and confident. Then you can have them **take 1 or 2 timed exams for practice before the actual test.**

If they can work on an exam just an hour a day, five out of seven days a week, all summer, they will improve tremendously and still have the entire day and night to attend any camp or have fun on vacation.

Remember: the learning takes place in going over the mistakes. If they don't review what they got wrong, they will NOT improve. This has to be done in a positive, constructive, non-punitive way.

There's no reason for frustration or anger over how many problems your child might get wrong on a practice test. **The more he gets wrong, the more he's going to improve**.

If they are having a tough time understanding why they got a problem wrong, and you cannot explain it to them, then that's when you might consider getting a tutor to go over the problems. But do not spend thousands of dollars on a tutor *just to have your child take a practice exam with the tutor!* Have your child take the exam on his or her own time at home and just review what he/she got wrong with the tutor. This will increase the value of your investment with the tutor.

Students should never take another practice exam without first going over the one they just finished so they can learn from their mistakes. If errors keep recurring on a particular type of question, keeping a notebook with these problems and their solutions for future review can be very helpful.

One mom I know spent thousands of dollars on SSAT and SAT tutoring for her child and did not see great results. The tutor would show her child how to work through a math problem by doing it for her, and then rave to the mom at the end of each session about smart her daughter was, how she could follow along as he showed her how to do the math problems. The mom and daughter naturally felt great after all the nice compliments, but unfortunately the daughter proceeded to fail both the SSAT and the SAT! What she needed instead was to work through these math problems on her own, over and over again, so that she was the one figuring out the solutions. It's fine not to know how to attack a problem; that's an opportunity for improvement! It's fine for a tutor to show a student how to do a problem, but then the student needs to practice doing those same types of problems on their own at home so they learn how do it themselves. No one will be there to help them on the exam!

If you are sending your kids to public high school and they don't have to take the SSAT, still have them take the practice exams anyway during the summer. The SSAT, like the SAT, tests the understanding of mathematical concepts, reading comprehension, and vocabulary. If your child can master these exams, he or she will have an extremely strong foundation and will likely excel in high school and on the college entrance exams.

Of course, the more reading they can do, the better. It really doesn't matter what they read, as long as they're reading. It will improve not only their vocabulary, but also their writing skills. If you have a child who doesn't love to read, taking the practice SSAT exams will have him reading short paragraphs and answering (around 5) questions about the reading, which will help keep him "up to speed."

***

The Best Ways to Study

Tips from Daniel Coyle's book, **The Talent Code: Greatness Isn't Born. It's Grown.**

In **The Talent Code**, Daniel Coyle discusses a study of a fifth grade class, in which the class was divided into two groups and given a handout to read. The students in the first group were allowed read the handout as many times as they wanted before being tested on the material. The students in the second group were only allowed to read the handout once before being quizzed on the handout. However, these students had to correct the quiz and then take another quiz on the same handout.

At the end of the study, a final test was given to all the students. The results showed that the kids who were quizzed repeatedly on the handout aced the exam, while the kids who studied the handout a lot more, but didn't take multiple quizzes, didn't score as well.

- **Quizzing yourself is the fastest way to learn information.** When your child has a vocabulary quiz, spelling test, or any other type of test, have either your child or his teacher (or you yourself) create a practice test with all the material on it. Have your child repeatedly take and correct the practice test (make sure the test gets corrected and reviewed before they try again). This should be done until the child is getting 100 percent correct.

    - **Mnemonics: A mnemonic is any learning technique that aids memory.** These can be associations, phrases, acronyms, or etc. If your child is having difficulty remembering something, try and come up with an association with the word, the sillier and more memorable the better.

    - **Mnemonic acronyms are great for lists.** For example, in middle school science they might have to memorize the eight classifications of organisms: Domain, Kingdom, Phylum, Class, Order, Family, Genius, and Species. A good mnemonic acronym could be: <u>D</u>umb <u>K</u>ids <u>P</u>laying <u>C</u>atch <u>O</u>n <u>F</u>reeways <u>G</u>et <u>S</u>quashed.

***

Your child should learn and memorize the top 400 middle school vocabulary words (attached below). The best way to memorize vocabulary is to follow this process:

1. Review all the words and separate those you know from those you either were unsure of or didn't know.

2. Make flash cards for all the words you don't know: put the word on the front and both the definition and one sentence using that word on the back.

3. Quiz yourself on the pile of note cards of words you didn't, putting the ones you get right in a separate pile. Keep quizzing yourself on the first pile (words you don't know or got wrong) until the pile disappears!

4. Then, every few days review all of the words and review any you don't remember.

You can also go to **quizlet.com** and type in a list of words and their definitions and then quiz yourself on the vocabulary with all kinds of games.

Use the summertime to learn and memorize these words. Vacations during the school year, when they don't have any homework, are also great times to have your child work on learning and memorizing words bit by bit.

Students could type up a quiz for themselves on 20 of the words that has them matching the word to the correct definition. The actual typing of the word and its definition will help learn the words. Then they can print several copies of this quiz to try and get 100 percent correct.

***

Have your child keep a file about each classic book they read in school. Also keep a file with a summary of historical information they learn in history classes. Save notes; keep a record of the title, author, and the themes in the books along with a few supporting examples. When it comes time to write the essay for the SSAT or the SAT, your child's score will soar if he or she includes an example from a book or history. Your child will save valuable time in high school if he or she starts this file in middle school.

***

Conclusion

Any child aiming for the Ivy League should have by the end of 8th grade:

1. Completed Algebra 1

2. Practiced and corrected as many SSAT exams as possible in the summer

3. Started taking Latin if your school offers it

4. Read as much as possible.

5. Spent time learning the top 400 vocabulary words for the SSAT exam.

The two most important things for your child to do would be finishing Algebra 1 and taking practice SSAT exams. If your child has mastered the SSAT in both the reading comprehension and math sections, they will be at the top of their class in terms of being ready for high school and beyond.

Remember, summer is the secret to getting ahead!

High School Years

Keys to Getting an Ivy League Acceptance

1. **Aim for an A or A- average**
   (requires a balanced course load!)
2. **Prepare for the SAT exam BEFORE junior year!**
3. **Get all SAT scores in the 700s.**
4. **Have SAT 2 scores in the 700s.**
5. **Get 5's on all AP exams.**
6. **Have a passion outside of the classroom (sports, music, art, community service, etc) that you have excelled in during your high school years.** Leadership roles are extremely valued.

***

Choosing a High School

When deciding on public versus private school, students should go to where they will thrive, not just survive. You want them to attend a school where they can possibly be in the top 5 to 10% of their class, especially if the student has a chance to be recruited by colleges for a sports team and still wants to go to a highly competitive academic college. When your child applies to a college, the name of the high school will usually only matter if the admissions office is on the fence about granting acceptance. If the high school's college advisory staff has a strong relationship with that particular college's admissions office, they may help influence the decision. There are many fantastic boarding schools ranked very high in the country, however, that do not have great relationships with many elite colleges.

One thing to consider is the balancing act that must occur: on the one hand attending an elite private school has prestige and cache that may very well prove useful, but on the other hand, it may be much harder to be in the top of the class at those elite private schools. Your child's competition when applying to the top colleges will be more difficult, moreover, because more students from these private schools will also be trying to get into those same highly competitive colleges.

I know a set of twins who chose different boarding schools. One went to a fairly average academic school, while the other went to one of the highest-ranked academic boarding schools in the country.

The student at the "less competitive" high school had a great 4 years, trying various sports, acting in plays, and enjoying a good social life on the weekends. She was easily accepted into Trinity College.

The other twin, who went to a top academic boarding school, had to work her butt off on homework every weekend and had little time for extracurricular activities. Where did this twin, the "smarter twin," get accepted as a result of all her extra hard work? She was eventually accepted off the wait list to Trinity College.

I mention these twins to illustrate how the "smarter" twin might have been a bigger fish than her sister, but she was in a much bigger pond at her prestigious prep school. She didn't get into any of the elite colleges because she was competing with so many other kids in her highly competitive high school. Her GPA was not as good as her twin's because her high school was harder and more rigorous. She ended up getting into the same college as her sister, but she had to get in off the waiting list while her sister was accepted directly!

I know another family who was so excited when their straight "A" middle school child got into one of the best boarding high schools in the country. The child did well academically there, but he was not in the top 15% of his class; he was a B+ student. When it came time to apply to college, his parents were stunned at the list of colleges the high school suggested: all 2nd and 3rd tier colleges. The parents felt that had they sent their son to a less competitive high school, he would have been at the top of his class and his list of prospective colleges would have looked much more impressive. I couldn't agree more!

I know of one athlete whose dream was to play at an Ivy League college, and so his parents sent him to a very academic boarding school, where he got low B's and C's. He had the athletic ability to play in the Ivies, but neither the GPA nor the Board scores. He was a poor test-taker, he was young for his grade, and he had not finished Algebra 1 before starting high school. Had his parents kept him back so that he could've completed Algebra 1 before high school, had he practiced as many SAT exams as possible during the summer after freshman year and sophomore year, and had he attended a high school where it would have been possible for him to get better grades, he likely could have achieved his goal of playing for an Ivy League college.

One student actually took a whole month off from school to do nothing but study for the SAT exam. While dedicated, his fatal flaw was that he only paid attention to the questions he got right! He never focused on any of the problems he got wrong and, lo and behold, his scores remained the same! He did take several practice exams, but he did not take them the right way. <u>Students must focus on what they get wrong in order to improve!</u>

On the other hand, a friend of mine worked hard enough to be accepted by and attend Middlebury College despite having a learning disability! His mother worked with him every summer during high school, solidifying his knowledge and practicing exams. It can be done! But, there's no free lunch. Put the time in on the practice exams, have students learn from their mistakes, and they can soar to new heights!

What Kind of Course Load Should My Child Take?

1. Students should **finish Algebra 1, Geometry, and Algebra 2** by the end of sophomore year.

2. No matter how advanced a student is, **do not overload on AP courses**! I know so many examples of smart kids loading their schedule with 4 or 5 AP's, involving themselves in extracurricular activities, and then seeing their GPA plummet as a result! **It is very important to maintain a high GPA, and a key for this is a balanced course load.**

My daughter took one AP sophomore year, 3 AP's junior year, and 2 AP's senior year, and struck a great balance with her course load. She was recruited by all of the Ivy League schools not only for her athletic ability, but also for her academic standing. On the other hand, I recently overheard two moms complaining that their sons were advised to take the most rigorous, impressive course load possible, only to find that other kids who had better balanced their course load ended up with better GPA's and better results when applying to college.

One student I know took a difficult course load in high school and did not have a strong GPA; she had a few C's on her transcript and a B- average. She scored pretty well but was rejected from Boston College while a few of her friends who had taken an easier course load, and thus gotten a higher GPA, were accepted!

GPA matters! It's not just board scores! Only allow students to take the number of AP courses that will enable them to work hard both inside and outside of the classroom and still achieve their highest possible GPA.

***

The College Entrance Exams (SAT & ACT)

Should a student take the ACT or SAT exam?

The SAT is more of a logic exam and the ACT is more straightforward. Typically, if your child is <u>not</u> a good test taker, the ACT will be easier for him or her. The ACT final score also averages the results from the four sections so that if your child is weaker in one subject and stronger in another, the stronger results from one section can help balance out the results from the weaker section in the final score.

Preparing

Michelle Obama was asked if she thought SAT exams were fair and she replied that at the present time, this is the system, so her best advice to students was to prepare for it!

The summer is the secret to being well prepared. The summer **before junior year** is the summer to go all out on preparing. Even if your child will be an athletic recruit, you don't want his or her first scores to be too low for a college he or she would like to attend. The coach might focus his recruiting efforts on someone else with better test scores and not wait for your child's senior year scores.

After sophomore year, practice SAT problems during the summer – have your student try and complete 8 exams so that when he or she takes the SAT or the ACT at the end of junior year, the homework for the exam has already been done. Everyone takes the SAT or ACT at the end of their junior year, but once the beginning of junior year starts in September, students will too busy with homework and after school activities to also study seriously for the board exams. They have to take advantage of the summer!

If you have a student who struggles with standardized, timed tests, then have that student start practicing SAT problems during the summer after *freshman* year and continue practicing them during the summer after sophomore year.

Students should start with the **College Board SAT study guide**. These problems might be slightly easier than the actual test, but it's a great place to start. **The Princeton Review** book has practice exams that are the same level as the problems on the actual exam. **The Barron's book** has practice exams that are the most difficult. **If your child is going for that perfect score, start with the College Board book, move on to the Princeton Review, and then finish off with the Barron's practice exams.**

In order to make a difference in board scores, **a student must complete 8 exams**! Ask the students who score in the 700's and almost all of them will say they practiced taking several exams. If a student wants to score well, he or she must put in the time and do the homework (in the form of practice exams). If they do, they will likely achieve their goal. Of course, **students MUST correct each practice exam and learn from the mistakes they made.**

One of the biggest mistakes parents make is assuming that if their child is a good student and/or attends a competitive private high school, they'll do fine on the SAT or the ACT. Even the combination of working very hard to maintain a high GPA, taking rigorous courses, and attending one of the most prestigious boarding schools in the country is not enough to guarantee success on the board exams. For the student who takes the summers off, a tutor for a just few weeks at the end of the summer, or during

Thanksgiving or Christmas break, will not have much of an impact. If you have a tutor for 2 weeks, you will not have time to complete 8 exams, not to mention reviewing them and learning from mistakes in order to improve. Remember: the learning and improving takes place in correcting the exams and learning from the incorrect problems. *If we do not learn from the past we are doomed to repeat it!*

Think about the students who go to a tutoring center and pay thousands of dollars for SAT prep. How many exams do they take? Are they going over every problem they get wrong and learning from them?

Now compare that preparation to that of students who completes 8 exams, corrects them, and reviews the mistakes they made. **You don't need to spend thousands of dollars for your child to be in a great position applying to the Ivy League.**

***

Practice exam tips:

I think breaking up the practice exams so that your student doesn't have to take a 3-hour exam in one sitting makes the whole task much less burdensome. After my daughter had finished a section or two of an exam, she had had enough and would take a break, and I would correct them later. The next day, instead of completing another section of the exam, she reviewed the problems she got wrong. If there's something that you think might be hard to remember, jot down some notes on a pad of paper to review a few days before the actual exam.

Also, it's not that important to time the practice exam. When my daughter started out practicing the math sections in June, she couldn't even finish one section in an hour and she would get a lot wrong! But by the end of August, after spending the summer reviewing her mistakes and learning to recognize the patterns, she was cruising through the math sections and getting only one or two problems wrong. She even commented during a practice section, "I know exactly what they're looking for in this problem!"

If students prepare all summer, and **complete 8 practice exams**, correcting each one and learning from their mistakes, they may very well not even have to take the SAT their senior year because they'll have already scored so well junior year.

On the ACT, the Science section typically gives most students trouble. Again, go to the bookstore or look on Amazon.com for ACT study guides and take as many practice exams as possible. **Practice is the key. Do not worry about how many you get wrong. The more you get wrong the bigger the opportunity you have to improve!**

***

Timing tips:

Finish practicing for the SAT or ACT exam by the start of a student's junior year. Use the summers after freshman and sophomore years to prepare. <u>Do not</u> count on students having the time to prepare for standardized exams during the school year.

Students will be taking the PSAT exam in October of their junior year. They will not have time to prepare once school starts in September. Prepare during the previous summer using the practice SAT exams. **SAT exams will prepare them for the PSAT exam, and they may also choose to order a couple of full-length PSAT exams on collegeboard.com to practice.**

Students should take the SAT in their junior year during the December or January tests because the SAT's are graded on a curve! Most seniors take the October test, and so the December and January tests are usually filled with those who did not do well on the October test and are trying again. It takes time to improve a score, and typically a student will be too busy with school and extracurricular activities to study between October and December/January enough to make a significant difference in their scores. This means that most of the students taking the December and January SAT's are going to get the same poor score that they were unhappy with the first time, which means a better curve.

May is also another good time to take the exam, as most advanced students will be busy taking AP exams during the time of the test, removing them from the grading pool and again giving your student a better curve. March and June, on the other hand, are not as good times to take the exam. These are the busiest test times, with lots of students taking the test, so they will usually have the toughest grade curves.

The January, May, and October tests are available to purchase after you take the test. Students can get the test booklet for a fee and then will be able to see exactly which questions they got wrong. Remember, the improving comes from correcting and learning from mistakes.

***

Tutoring Tips:

I know a mom whose son did not do well in Algebra 1, and so she was thinking of sending him to summer school to retake Algebra 1 so that he would not just get a better grade, but really understand the material. However, math books often operate by teaching a mathematical rule followed by several straightforward problems showing the application of that rule. Taking SAT practice exams, on the other hand, is a much better strategy, because these exams zero in on fundamental understanding of the concepts. In fact, SAT math problems often involve several mathematical variables and concepts in one problem, so the student must understand the theory behind the rules in order to solve them. **Practicing SAT math problems thus teaches students a mastery of the concepts,** rather than just an understanding of how to solve a specific problem. Working on these SAT problems is the fastest method to help students improve and gain confidence. In other words, if your child practices 800 SAT math problems, goes over why they got problems wrong, and learns how to arrive at the correct answer, he or she is going to improve in math!

The importance of learning from these practice sections means that you have to take the following approach regarding SAT tutors or else risk wasting time and money: **<u>Do not pay for a tutor to simply have your child take the practice tests.</u>** If you or your child wants to go to a tutor, you must ask the tutor, "How many practice tests will my child take," "Who will correct them," and "How will the wrong answers be reviewed with the student?" Have your child take the practice tests at home and then use the tutor to go over the problems he or she got wrong. This is the only way to make sure that the time spent with a tutor is an efficient, productive use of time and money.

For example, there is one company selling themselves as tutors for Ivy League admission, offering to go to your child's boarding school and do SAT prep on several Saturday's throughout the fall term. They charge thousands of dollars, but simply have their students spend the entire time taking practice exams, not reviewing and learning from incorrect answers. Not surprisingly, very little improvement is accomplished. What is surprising is that parents actually pay for this at all!

Bottom line: save the tutors for going over problems that your child gets wrong or doesn't understand, not for taking the exam. In other words, use the tutor as a teaching tool to fill in any gaps in understanding, not as a babysitter!

***

Tips on the writing section from a high-priced SAT writing coach who also is a grader of the actual essays:

As briefly mentioned previously, having students keep a file containing each classic book they read in school, along with another one for historical information they learn in history classes, provides a clutch resource when preparing for the SAT's. The student should keep a record of the title, author, the themes of the books, and a few examples that support those themes. When students write the essay on the SAT or the SSAT, their scores will soar if they can include an example from a classic book or from history. Your child will save time in high school if he/she starts to keep these notes in Middle School. Please refer to the Writing section near the end of this book for more detailed advice on the essay.

***

Tips for Other Exams:

The same advice goes for the **AP exams** and **SAT 2 subject test exams**: PREPARE by taking practice exams! Students should take as many as they can.

If a student is home schooled, make sure he/she completes the syllabus for all AP courses at least 2 weeks before the exam in May so that he/she has time to take practice exams.

When my daughter took an AP course in high school sophomore year, the teacher made sure the students finished the syllabus well before the end of school so that students had time for practice exams and review. Many distance-learning programs, however, do not emphasize the importance of finishing the course work 2 weeks before the exam. My daughter was home schooled for her junior and senior years of high school, and that would be one of my few criticisms: home school programs often don't make sure you finish the course 2 weeks before the AP exam so that you have time to prepare to score really well.

***

Setting Your Sights

It is often a good idea to go to the college advisor at your child's high school, ask about previous students who applied to some of the schools you and your child may have an eye on, and make a list of attributes of the students who were accepted. **Doing this early on might help focus your child during their high school years and give both you and your child a clear understanding of what it will take, coming out of your particular high school, to be accepted by some of these colleges.**

Too often, parents and students assume that with an A average, they will automatically be in contention for spots at the top colleges. Parents need to understand that high school college advisors are often assigned up to 35 students, and, as the saying goes, "The squeaky wheel gets the oil." You have to be an active advocate for your child with your high school's college advisors. Learn what your child will need to emphasize on his or her college application for a particular school. Ask the college advisor about contacting a college coach or music director or etc on behalf of your child.

***

Potential Ivy League Athletes

If your child is an athlete that would like to play for one of the Ivy League schools, he/she will need **at least a score of 600 on each section of the SAT's and have a strong GPA. Athletes have been told that a "C" in any subject on a transcript is like cancer.** Some Ivy League schools have a minimum requirement of a score of 650 or better in each subject. It depends on the sport and on the school, but a general rule of thumb is a score of 600 per section at the minimum. To be honest, the Ivy League colleges are like other schools in that they want the best athletes. If your son or daughter is a top-notch athlete, the coach will try to get him/her and should be successful as long the student has a solid GPA without C's and a score of 600 or better on each section of the SAT. The student doesn't necessarily even need to have taken any AP courses! If you're wondering how good of an athlete you have to be in order to get recruited, **go to a few Ivy League college websites and read the bios of the athletes on the team.** Typically, the better the athlete, the more the admissions office is willing to overlook any academic shortcomings, as long as the athlete still meets the minimum requirements.

***

Non-Athletes: The Myth of Being Well-Rounded

If your child is not an athlete, he or she needs to aim for scores in the 700's on each section of the SAT exam and should be in the top 5 – 10% of his or her class.

The application also needs to show commitment to an outside interest along with a great GPA and great board scores. Passion and excellence are required.

Students need to use the summers to enhance their resume with training or leadership roles. Doing something productive with their summer that's going to help them be unique, something that will demonstrate a passion about something outside of the classroom. This will make their application stand out to Ivy League Admission officers. **Students need to be able to stand out among all the other students applying with the same (or better) GPA's and board scores.**

In 2011, Harvard accepted the smallest percentage of applicants in its history, and it **routinely turns down over 1000 students per year with perfect SAT scores**. Students must have something special, a unique quality, in addition to their good grades and high board scores. Simply being great academically is not enough. If they're not going to play a sport in college, students should concentrate on music or art or some other talent, and then also have them get involved in a charity or community service project where they **can take a leadership role.** Instead of trying to do a lot of things well, choose one area to be the best you can be. Students need one really good quality, besides their great grades and SAT scores, to make the cut.

Colleges do not want well-rounded individuals; they want a well-rounded student body.

National recognition really makes a student's application stand out. So, if a student is NOT going to be a Division I athlete, start freshman year with involvement in something for which they can earn national recognition. Or find a charity in which they can develop a leadership role over the course of their 4 years in high school.

Colleges can see right through a candidate who only volunteers for a few weeks one summer. This does not show the passion, commitment, or leadership that the Ivy League colleges are looking for. It instead smacks of application window dressing.

On the college application essay, think of the reader. An admissions officer has to sit and read through thousands of essays. Students need to write an interesting story that will help the reader get to know them and makes them unforgettable and unique. In their essay for their college application, students should try and tell a story that centers on their strongest accomplishments. **Admissions officers LOVE stories!** Students need to tell a story that allows the admissions officer to get to know their strengths, insights, etc. Students should try and write an essay that shows how their experience has made them who they are.

Some current freshmen in my daughter's dorm at Harvard:

- A national scrabble champion
- A national spelling champion
- An international mathematician

- Athletes of various sports
- A person who did the debate team and mock trial in high school
- An organizer of a charity that was very successful
- A student who described himself as "pretty relatively average" so he joined the school's choir, was on the Honor Council, became captain of his school's tour guides, participated in the school musical, volunteered at his local soup kitchen, spent a summer working as an intern at the Villanova law school, and spent another summer working in Madrid at an adoption agency. This student's resume sounds impressive, but he was just a normal guy with no outstanding talent so he got his hands on everything he could (but real, meaningful commitments) and stood out as a result.

Thus the key to Ivy League admission is the combination of a solid GPA, high SAT scores, and "something else" in which the candidate has excelled. When asked the most common theme among students at Harvard, Harvard freshmen consistently responded, "**Everyone has one thing they're really good at**." An application will stand out if the student expresses an interest in which he or she has achieved significant recognition, or if the student has had a major positive impact on society in some way. Admissions officers are looking for the best students in every facet of life. A well-rounded student with a great GPA and great board scores, but without excellence in any one particular area, will most likely be turned down by the Ivy League Colleges. **In fact, Ivy League colleges would rather accept the student with strong academic numbers and passion/excellence displayed in another area than the student with only perfect academic scores.**

<u>However:</u> Students should not try to be involved in <u>so</u> many things that they cannot possibly be great at any one of them! As the saying goes, "**Jack of all trades, master of none.**" The top schools are looking for the masters.

***

Conclusion
High school in a nutshell

Make sure students have completed Algebra 1, Geometry and Algebra 2 by the end of their sophomore year.

Students should **take Latin** as a language to improve their vocabulary and grammar. Students who haven't taken Latin and/or are struggling on the practice exams with any vocabulary, **get the Princeton Review SAT book or the Princeton Review Word Smart books and work through a list of words.**

Have students devote the summer before junior year to taking, completing and correcting at least 8 full length SAT or ACT exams. If a student is not a good test taker, have him/her start practicing the summer after freshman year.

Students should not aim to be good at everything. They need to try and find a passion where they focus on excelling in that one thing. They need their college application to stand out.

Make sure your child is involved in an activity during the summer in a particular area that they are passionate about. Great grades and great SAT scores are not enough these days to make your application stand out. Everyone applying to the top colleges will have those credentials. What will make your child stand out? Figure out what they are interested in and have them get involved during their summers.

Any **national recognition** they can achieve will definitely make their application shine. Along with good grades and strong board scores, they want something that makes them special: nationally ranked athlete, national essay contest winner, nationally recognized musician, artist, singer, debate, etc. Instead of just being involved in a charity, students should look for **leadership roles** in the organization.

Encourage your child to participate in classes and to realize how important teacher recommendations will be in the application process. Teacher recommendations do play an important role. I have not discussed this fact simply because if your child is aiming at the Ivy League and going for the A's, I'm assuming your child's teacher recommendations naturally are going to be strong

Among best parenting advice I have received was to **keep your teenagers busy**. While it is important for them to have down time and to socialize, during the high school years they need to be kept as busy as possible. Idle hands often find trouble. For that reason alone, I know some parents who purposely picked a very rigorous high school to keep their children busy and out of trouble.

***

A Final Word on Star Power

As previously discussed, one of the myths about private high school is that attending one automatically makes a student do better on standardized exams. Another myth is that a great GPA will be enough to get accepted into the top colleges since they are coming from an elite private high school. These beliefs couldn't be further from the truth!

Most private schools **do not prepare your child well for standardized exams**, nor do they work on his/her resumes. **Students must not only succeed in the classroom, but they must also be accomplished in something other than academics in order to get into the best colleges.**

As a parent, you want to guide your children so that their college application will show their best possible GPA, their highest possible SAT score, and then something else besides academics that they have succeeded in either on large scale or that shows their great impact on a community. In today's hypercompetitive world, a student needs this something else, this shine factor, star power, golden gift, or silver separator. Imagine your child's college application in a large pile with many others containing the same GPA and board scores. You want to make sure there is something about your son or daughter's application that makes it stand out.

One girl I know traveled to Africa and was so moved by seeing a village full of children who couldn't afford to go to school, that she started making and selling bead necklaces. She sent all the proceeds to the village and has now helped educate hundreds of children in that African village!

Another girl I know of went to a very prestigious, top-rated boarding school, had an overall average of 94%, and scored in the high 600's on each section of the SAT's, yet she did not get into any of the most selective colleges in the United States! The reason was because she wrote her application essay about how her immigrant father had come from nothing and worked very hard to achieve great success in the United States. The only problem was that her father was not applying to college! Her essay made her father sound great, but failed to highlight her own strengths. She came off like a very wealthy girl who was spoiled, writing that her major interest besides making sure she got good grades was shopping.

Her parents were devastated at her college acceptance results. There are hundreds of kids for few spots, all with the same good grades and board scores. She had nothing else on her application except traveling and volunteering at a retirement center for only a few hours one summer.

Knowing she was not interested in playing a college sport, her parents should have made sure she had made a significant impact as a leader in some charity, or something other than socializing every summer at the beach and taking lavish family vacations!

This girl was so confident academically, she felt she didn't need any advice and even refused to let her parents look at her college essay before submitting it.

Always have your child's essay reviewed by as many people as you can, whether by parents, teachers, college advisors, or etc. Make sure your child gets someone else's input on the essay!

What about the student who has great grades, strong SAT's scores, and plays sports in high school but is not good enough to play at the college level? What should that student do to make a shining application?

In the above case, I would recommend that that student first investigate how good at their sport they need to be in order to play at a Division III college. Contacting a Division III coach and letting them know of your interest in playing for them can accelerate acceptance! If the student is not at the Division III level, however, then I would recommend they continue to play the sport in high school for health and enjoyment, but to also think about ways to utilize his or her summers. What could that student do, perhaps in terms of a charity, where they could take on a leadership role? What impressive internship could they do that would demonstrate hard work and valuable experience? Does the high school have a debate or mock trial team the student could join and possibly advance to a state or national competition? Whatever they choose, it needs to be a legitimate commitment to make them stand out.

If your child has a particular strength but is not interested in continuing in college, still emphasize that attribute on his/her college application! One student I know at one of the top boarding schools in the country was an extremely talented violin player. She made the state orchestra without much practice at all and was clearly a very gifted musician. But since she decided she didn't want to continue playing in college, she merely just listed her involvement in the state orchestra on her application like it was not a big deal. This was a mistake; she did not receive the proper advice from her high school's college placement office on how to strengthen her application by emphasizing her talents, and she was subsequently rejected by many schools. And wouldn't you know, now she's in college and misses her violin; now she wants to play! A sharp college placement officer would have called a contact at the college or university to let them know about this student and her amazing talent with the violin!

Contacting a Division III coach, music department head, or other person at the college or university and getting their support for your child's application is a good move. It does NOT force you to play that sport or instrument when you get to that college, but it may help your child gain acceptance there!

In fact, I know many students who have used a talent to get into college and then promptly changed their mind about participating once they got there! That is a fair and legal move. If your child put in the work and practice throughout high school, then he or she should get the credit for it during the college application process.

The lesson here is students should use **EVERYTHING** they have to get into college!

The more people I interviewed in my research for this book, the more I came to realize that many college placement advisors in many of the best schools do not advise each student about how to emphasize their strengths on the application. They do not demand that the student has someone give them feedback on their application essay. They do not help them understand how and when they need to study for the SAT's and what they should be trying to accomplish during the summers. I've even heard some schools say students don't need to study for the SAT because their curriculum prepares them sufficiently! That is the furthest thing from the truth. There's always an exception to the rule, but for the most part, all students need to prepare for the SAT's.

As a parent, my advice is to get involved! Go to your college advisor and specifically ask about your child's chances of getting into the colleges he/she is interested in, and what he/she can do to maximize that possibility. Get advice on the essay, the interview, and emphasizing the student's strengths. Ask what he/she can do to make his/her application stand out. Students should email the college coach or the head of the orchestra or whomever. Get a recommendation from an alumnus if possible. Ask the college placement office which schools they have the strongest relationship with to possibly make a push for your child. Definitely have students visit the school and sign in! Visits show that students are serious about attending that university or college.

To summarize the advice from this Harvard mom, constantly look for how you can put your children in the best position to succeed. Have them work hard and work smart. Make good decisions about when and how to study. **Try to develop a talent that will garner recognition at the state, national, or even international level, and make sure colleges know about it.** An application has to sell itself, this is not the time for modesty: encourage and support your child to be the absolute best that he or she can be. And above all else, be happy and proud of your child when they are giving their best, whatever that may be and wherever that make take them. May God bless you as you travel the long, winding, wonderful path from preschool to success!

***

Math Review for the SAT Exam

This review is taken from a research project on SAT math on what our math books don't review or review enough.

This review is for the students who have already gone over the basic math review sections in any study guide: College Board, Princeton Review, or Barron's.

These are the finer tips for the math section.

A review of problems or topics for the student trying for the perfect score on the math section.

Sometimes a student can be so strong in math that by junior year of high school, they are already in Calculus and some are even in Calculus 2!

The problem they face on the SAT's is that the SAT exam only covers math through Algebra 2 and it has been a couple of years since they have had to solve Algebra 2 problems.

Even for those advanced math students, they need to prepare by taking at least 8 exams. I know several strong math students who scored in the low 600's the first time on the SAT exam because of this very reason.

WORK RATE PROBLEMS

REMEMBER : When solving work rate problems:

1. Find the unit rate

2. Add the unit rates together to see how much work they do together

3. Set up a ratio

Example:

One machine makes 300 bolts per hour. A new machine makes 450 bolts per hour. If both machines begin running at the same time, how many minutes will it take the two machines to make 900 bolts?

Solution:

1. The information is already given in the unit rate. You are told that the first machine makes 300 bolts per 1 hour and the new machine makes 450 bolts per 1 hour.

2. Adding the unit rates together: 300 + 450 = 750 bolts/hr working together.

3. Set up the ratio:

$$\frac{750 \text{ bolts}}{1 \text{ hour}} = \frac{900 \text{ bolts}}{x \text{ hours}}$$

Cross multiplying you get: 750 x = 900

Divide both sides by 750 to get: x = 1.2 hours

So, they'll make 900 bolts in 1.2 hours.

Remember – the question asked for the answer in minutes!

$$1.2 \text{ hours} \times \frac{60 \text{ minutes}}{1 \text{ hour}} = 72 \text{ minutes}$$

(Remember, when converting units, always put the unit you want to cancel in the denominator)

Example: (question on an actual SAT)

If Jan shovels the walk in 4 minutes, Michael shovels the walk in 3 minutes, how long will it take them to shovel the walk together?

Solution:

1. **Find the unit rate.**

We're told Jan shovels 1 walk in 4 minutes.

So, in 1 minute, she'll have shoveled ¼ of the walk.

Michael will shovel 1/3 of the walk in 1 minute.

2. **Add the rates together:**

¼ + 1/3 = 3/12 + 4/12 = 7/12

Together they will shovel 7/12 of the walk in 1 minute.

3. **Set up the ratio:**

$$\frac{7/12 \text{ walk}}{1 \text{ minute}} = \frac{1 \text{ walk}}{x \text{ minutes}}$$

Cross multiply: 7/12 x = 1 walk

Divide by 7/12 to get:

x = 12/7 minutes   or 1 5/7 minutes to shovel 1 walk.

***

Question:

Jan mows her lawn in 60 minutes, Wally can mow the lawn in 30 minutes, and Peter can mow the lawn in 40 minutes.

If Jan starts moving for 15 minutes, then Wally and Peter help her finish, how long will it take in hours?

Here is one the more involved work rate problems.

If you can understand and solve this, the problems with two people or two machines will seem easy.

Notice they give you the information in minutes but ask for the answer in hours.

There are two ways to solve the problem; you can either convert how much they mow in minutes to hours first, or you can find out how long it takes for them to mow in minutes first and then convert the number to hours.

Both ways are shown:

First: find the unit rate:

(Calculating the unit rate in hours)

You're given how many minutes it takes to mow one lawn but asked for the answer in hours.

First: Find out how many lawns they can each mow in 1 hour (the unit rate).

Second: Find out how many lawns they mow together in 1 hour.

Last: Set up a ratio to find out how long it will take.

Hint: If Jan mows alone for 15 min, then you need to find out how long it will take the three of them mowing together to mow ¾ of a lawn and then add 15 min or ¼ of an hour.

(Remember, Jan mows the whole lawn in 60 min, so she'll have mowed ¼ of lawn in 15 min)

Given: Jan mows 1 lawn in 1 hour.

In 15 minutes, she'll have mowed ¼ of the lawn.

Given: Peter mows 1 lawn in 2/3 hour.

Find the unit rate: How much does he mow in 1 hour?

$$\frac{1 \text{ lawn}}{2/3 \text{ hr}} = \frac{x \text{ lawns}}{1 \text{ hour}} \quad \text{Cross multiply:}$$

$1 = 2/3x$ Multiply both sides by 3/2 to solve for x.

$x = 3/2$ lawns in one hour.

Peter can mow 3/2 lawns in 1 hour.

Given:

<u>Wally can mow 1 lawn in 30 minutes</u> or 2 lawns in 1 hour.

<u>Working together:</u>

To find out how much they can mow working together,

add how much they each mow in one hour:

Adding Wally + Peter + Jan:

2 + 3/2 + 1 = 4/2 + 3/2 + 2/2 = 9/2 lawns will be mowed working together in 1 hour.

Set up your ratio: How long will it take 3 people to mow ¾ of a lawn?

$$\frac{9/2 \text{ lawns}}{1 \text{ hour}} = \frac{3/4 \text{ lawns}}{x \text{ hour}}$$

Cross multiply to get: 9/2 x = ¾

Divide by 2/9 to solve:

x = (2/9)(3/4) = 6/36 = 1/6

It will take 1/6 of an hour for all three to mow ¾ of the lawn.

The questions asks how long it will take to mow the lawn if Jan mows for 15 minutes and then Wally and Peter help her finish, so don't forget to add the 15 minutes!

Jan already mowed for ¼ of an hour so (¼ + 1/6) =

(3/12 + 2/12) =

5/12 of an hour for one lawn to be mowed.

So, with Jan mowing for the first fifteen minutes and Wally and Peter helping her finish, it will take 5/12 of an hour.

There is another way to solve this problem.

First: Find the unit rate in minutes: (instead of hours)

How much does each person mow in 1 minute:

Jan mows 1 lawn in 60 minutes so she'll mow 1/60 of a lawn in 1 minute.

Peter mows 1 lawn in 40 minutes so he'll mow 1/40 of a lawn in 1 minute.

Wally mows 1 lawn in 30 minutes so he'll mow 1/30 of a lawn in 1 minute.

Second: Find out how much they mow together by adding what they each mow:

Together they mow 1/60 + 1/40 + 1/30 =

(find a common denominator)

2/120 + 3/120 + 4/120 =

9/120 of a lawn in 1 minute.

Third, set up the ratio:

$$\frac{9/120 \text{ lawn}}{1 \text{ min}} = \frac{3/4 \text{ lawn}}{x \text{ min}}$$

Cross multiply: (9/120) x = ¾

Now, multiply by 120/9 to solve for x:

(3/4)(120/9)

(which reduces to):

(1/1)(30/3)

(4 divides into 120, 30 times and 3 divides into 9, 3 times)

(1/1)(30/3) = 30/3 or

10 minutes for the three of them to mow ¾ of the lawn.

Add the 15 min Jan mowed by herself, and you get 25 minutes.

Last: Now you have to convert 25 minutes to hours:

$$\frac{25 \text{ min}}{x \text{ hr}} = \frac{60 \text{ min}}{1 \text{ hour}}$$

Cross multiply:

25 = 60x

Divide by 60

25/60 = 5/12 hour

***

Part-to-Part Ratio

When given an part-to-part ratio (not part to whole),

the total number of items must be a multiple of the total number of items.

Example: The ratio of teachers to students is 1 to 10,

What could be the total number of teachers and students?

A) 100

B) 121

C) 144

D) 222

E) 1, 011

Answer B, 121

A multiple of both numbers added together, 11, which is the total number of items:

teachers + students = 10 + 1 = 11

Another Example:

A ratio of white eggs in a basket to brown eggs is 2:3.

What is the total number of eggs in the basket?

The answer must be a multiple of 5!

A) 12

B) 14

C) 20

D) 6

The correct answer is 20: the only multiple of 5.

***

YOU CANNOT ADD OR SUBTRACT FROM PARTS OF A RATIO, BUT YOU CAN MULTIPLY AND DIVIDE!!!

Example:

A ratio is 3:4.

If each quantity is increased by 1, what is the new ratio?

The trap is adding one to each part of the ratio and picking 4:5.

The correct answer to this question is:

Cannot determine from the information given!!

***

Parts of different ratios don't always refer to the same whole.

Example:

The ratio of quarters to dimes is 5:2.

The ratio of dimes to nickels is 3:4.

What's the ratio of quarters to nickels?

Since the two ratios <u>do not refer to the same amount of dimes,</u> students must rewrite the ratios so they will refer to the same amount of dimes:

Multiply (5 quarters to 2 dimes) by 3 to get 15 quarters to 6 dimes or 15:6.

Multiply (3 dimes to 4 nickels) by 2 to get 6 dimes to 8 nickels or 6:8.

Now you have the ratio of quarters to dimes is 15:6.

The ratio of dimes to nickels is 6:8.

Both ratios refer to 6 dimes.

Now you can compare the quarters to nickels: 15:8.

***

PROPORTION

Make sure when you set up a proportion, you have the same units on the top on both sides of the equation.

You also need the same units on the bottom on both sides of the equation.

If $\dfrac{a}{b} = \dfrac{c}{d}$

Which is NOT true?

1) $\dfrac{ad}{bc} = \dfrac{1}{1}$

2) $\dfrac{a}{c} = \dfrac{b}{d}$

3) $\dfrac{c}{a} = \dfrac{d}{b}$

4) $\dfrac{d}{c} = \dfrac{b}{a}$

5) $\dfrac{a}{d} = \dfrac{b}{c}$

Try and figure this problem out before looking at the solution.

You can figure this out mathematically:

Remember, we're looking for the choice that does NOT work:

Cross Multiply to get :

ad = bc.

1. Dividing both sides by bc :   ad/bc = 1. Choice 1 works.

2. You can divide both sides of ad = bc, by c and then by d to see that choice 2 is correct:

3. You divided both sides of ad = bc, by a and then by b, to see that choice 3 is correct.

4. If you divided both sides by c and then by a, you see that choice 4 is correct.

5. The only equation you cannot get is the fifth choice,

so that is the correct choice.

There is another way to solve this problem:

You could also have substituted any numbers into the original equation: by picking any two fractions that are equal:

For example:

$$\frac{3}{6} = \frac{1}{2}$$

Now, you could test out the different ratios to see which ones are true:

1. (3)(2) / (6)(1) = 1   Yes

2. 3/1 = 6/2   Yes

3. 1/3 = 2/6   Yes

4. 2/1 = 6/3   Yes

5. 3/2 does NOT = 6/1   Choice 5 is the correct choice.

***

Consecutive Integers:

Memorize the sum of consecutive integers formula:

(n/2)(n +1) where n = the number of integers

Example:

What is the sum of the first 30 positive integers?

Solution:

15(31) = 465

NOTICE – STUDENTS MUST KNOW THAT <u>POSITVE INTEGERS</u> DO NOT INCLUDE 0!

IF THEY DON'T KNOW THIS, THEY MIGHT use n = 31 INSTEAD OF 30 AND GET THE WRONG ANSWER.

***

ALSO – KNOW THAT THE AVERAGE OF EVENLY SPREAD NUMBERS = THE AVERAGE OF THE SMALLEST + LARGEST:

Example:

What is the average of the first 30 positive integers?

Solution:

The first 30 positive integers starts with 1 and ends with 30.

The smallest number = 1

The largest = 30

(1 + 30)/ 2 = 15.5

***

FUNCTIONS

Remember to use the <u>equation of slope</u> to find points on a line.

$$\text{Slope} = \frac{y_2 - y_1}{x_2 - x_1}$$

For example:

If the slope = 2/3 and a point (6,8) is on the line, and another point has an X-coordinate of 4, find the unknown y-coordinate (4, y).

Solution:

Plug the numbers into the slope formula:

You would solve: $2/3 = \frac{8-y}{6-4}$

$$2/3 = \frac{(8-y)}{2}$$

Multiply both sides by 2:

4/3 = 8 - y

Add y to both sides and subtract 4/3 from both sides to get: Y = 8 – 4/3

Rewrite 8 as 24/3 to get a common denominator:

y = 24/3 – 4/3

y = 20/3 or 6 2/3

***

Remember: If a point is on a line, it solves the equation of that line.

For example:

If a line passes through the origin and is perpendicular to the line 4x + y = k, and the two lines intersect at (t, t + 1), what is the value of t?

Solution:

First: you must know that the slope of the unknown line will be the negative reciprocal of the slope of line 4x + y = k because it is perpendicular to this line.

You must also know the equation of a line, y = mx + b where m is the slope.

So, rewrite the given line in this format to find the slope:

Given: 4x + y = k

Rewrite: y = - 4x + k

The slope of the given line is: - 4.

The slope of the line perpendicular to it will be ¼

(the negative reciprocal).

(Whenever you're given an equation for a line, you know the slope of the line perpendicular to it because it is the negative reciprocal of that slope.)

Second: You must realize that you were given two points on the line:

1. the origin (0,0) 2. (t , t + 1)

Now, knowing two points and the slope you can calculate the value of t using the equation of slope and two points:

$$\text{Slope} = \frac{y_2 - y_1}{x_2 - x_1}$$

$$\frac{1}{4} = \frac{t + 1 - 0}{t - 0} \quad \text{or}$$

$$\frac{1}{4} = (t+1)/t$$

Now, you can solve for t.

Multiply both sides by t: (get rid of the denominator)

t/4 = t + 1

Multiply both sides by 4) t = 4t + 4

Subtract both sides by 4t) -3t = 4

Divide both sides by -3) t = - 4/3

***

Know: What happens to the graph of a linear equation when a negative number is multiplied to the slope.

***

Know: What happens to a graph with the slope of 1 when it is multiplied by 2.

***

Example:

The graph of $x = y^2 - 4$ intersects line L at (0,p) and (5,t):

What is the greatest possible slope?

Solution:

Students can find the Greatest Possible Slope of the line L by:

first plugging in the <u>points into the equation</u> to find the values of p and t.

(since the points are on that line, they satisfy the equation)

$x = y^2 - 4$

Plug in (0,p):

$0 = p^2 - 4$ (add 4 to both sides)

$4 = p^2$ (square root both sides)

$p = \pm 2$

Plug in (5,t):

$5 = t^2 - 4$

$9 = t^2$

$\pm 3 = t$

Now you can find the greatest possible slope by plugging in the values $(0, \pm 2)$ and $(5, \pm 3)$ into the equation to find slope:

Our values: (0,2) (0,-2) and (5,3)(5,-3)

$$\text{Slope} = \frac{y_2 - y_1}{x_2 - x_1}$$

Using (5, 3) and (0, 2):   3 – 2/5 – 0   = 1/5

Using (5, - 3) and (0, 2): -3 – 2/ 5 - 0   = -5/5 = -1

Using (5, -3) and (0, -2): -3 – (-2)/ 5 – 0 = -1/5

Using (5, 3) and (0, -2):   3 – (-2)/5 – 0 = 5/5 = 1:

The greatest possible slope is 1.

***

If a point intersects two lines, it satisfies both equations.

For example:

$(\sqrt{6}, k)$ is a point of intersection of graphs $y = x^2 - 7$ and $y = (-x^2 + J)$ where J is a constant.

What is the value of J?

Solution:

Plug in ($\sqrt{6}$, k) into the first equation to solve for K: (You can't plug in ($\sqrt{6}$, k) into the second equation because then you'd have two unknown variables, k and J).

First equation: $y = -x^2 - 7$

Plug into the first equation:

$k = (\sqrt{6})^2 - 7$
$= 6 - 7 = -1.$

Now you have the value of x and y,

$(\sqrt{6}, -1)$

and can solve for J in the second by plugging these values into the equation:

$y = (-x^2 + J)$

$-1 = -(\sqrt{6})^2 + J$
$-1 = -6 + J$
$5 = J$

***

The slope of a line will be the same for ANY two points on the line.
Use the slope formula to solve problems:

Example:

Given the values of a linear function f, (0,a), (1,24), (2,b), solve for a + b.

Solution:

First realize what you're given; three points for a linear function.

All three points are on the same line so they all have the same slope.

So, calculating the slope between these two points (0,a) and (1,24) will be the same as calculating the slope between the other two points (1, 24) and (2,b):

$$\text{Slope} = \frac{y_2 - y_1}{x_2 - x_1}$$

Using: (0, a) and (1, 24) and setting it equal to the slope using points (1, 24) and (2, b):

$$\frac{24 - a}{1 - 0} = \frac{24 - b}{1 - 2} \quad \text{or} \quad \frac{24 - a}{1} = \frac{24 - b}{-1}$$

Cross Multiply to get:

$-24 + a = 24 - b$

Add 24 to both sides and add b to both sides:

$a + b = 48$.

Realize that you might not be able to solve for the value of a and the value of b, only the value of a + b.

***

Solving for an unknown value, a variable, for a function:

Example:

If $f(x) = 2x - 1$ and $(1/2) f(\sqrt{t}) = 4$, what is the value of t?

Solution:

Substitute $\sqrt{t}$ for x in $f(x) = 2x - 1$ and then multiply the result by ½ to get:
½[(2√t) – 1] = 4

Multiply both sides by 2:
2√t – 1 = 8

Add 1 to both sides:
2√t = 9

Divide both sides by 2:
√t = 9/2

Square both sides to isolate the t: t = 81/4

***

Finding the value of a function with a variable is very similar to finding the value of a function for a number:

If you have a problem that asks for the value of F(2m) or F(m + 3), you simply plug in the value 2m for x in the function or plug in the value m + 3 for x.

***

A point on a graph satisfies the equation for that graph, so if there are any unknown values in the equation, knowing one point will allow you to solve for that variable.

Example:

Point (1, 3) is on $y = ax^2$, what's the value of a?

Solution:

Simply plug in (1, 3) into $y = ax^2$ and you get:

$$3 = a(1)^2$$
$$3 = a$$

***

Students must be able to identify the graph of a linear function with a negative slope and a positive y-intercept.

Students might be shown two graphs with a negative slope.

One will cross the y-axis at y = 0 and the other will cross at

y = 3.

The SAT question will ask, which graph has a positive y intercept?

The answer is the graph with y = 3.

***

Know:

Zero is neither positive nor negative!!!

***

Know the movement of graphs:

Students could be shown a graph called f(x) and <u>not told the equation of the graph.</u>

They will have to choose the graph that is f(x + 2).

Know that the function will have moved 2 units to the left.

Just as the function f(x − 2), the graph will have moved 2 units to the right.

***

Be comfortable with solving a function for a variable:

Example:

Given $h(x) = \dfrac{14 + x^2}{4}$

if $h(2m) = 9m$, what is one possible value of m?

Solution:

Plug in 2m for x in the given equation:

$H(2m) = \dfrac{14 + (2m)^2}{4}$

$= \dfrac{14 + 4m^2}{4}$

$= 14 + m^2$

Solve: $9m = 14 + m^2$
$0 = m^2 - 9m + 14$
$= (m - 7)(m - 2)$
$m = 7, m = 2$

Example:

What is the value of m if $f(2m) = 2f(m)$ for the function: $f(x) = x^2 + 18$?

Solution:

Plug in 2m for x and set it equal to the equation when you plug m in for x and multiply the result by 2.

$(2m)^2 + 18 = 2(m^2 + 18)$

$4m^2 + 18 = 2m^2 + 36$

$2m^2 = 18$

$m^2 = 9$

$m = 3$

***

QUADRATIC EQUATIONS:

STUDENTS DO NOT NEED TO KNOW THE QUADRATIC FORMULA BUT THEY DO NEED TO UNDERSTAND QUADRATIC EQUATIONS:

FOR EXAMPLE:

Given a graph of a quadratic function and told its maximum value is H(2) and at H(A) = 0, which could be the value of A?

Solution:

Because H(2) is the graphs maximum value, we know that the line x = 2 is the **Axis of Symmetry** for the graph.

The axis of symmetry, x = 2, means that the graph will cross the x-axis more than 2 units from 2, so A must be greater than 2.

You can see from this question that without giving you the equation of the graph, they test your knowledge of the Axis of Symmetry and a Quadratic Graph.

***

SOLVING A QUADRATIC EQUATION GIVEN THE HEIGHT OF AN OBJECT:

This is an involved problem and would be at the end of a math section and for those students going for the 800.

Example:

Given the equation $H(t) = C - (d - 4t)^2$.

At $t = 0$, a ball was thrown upward from an initial height of 6 feet. It reached its maximum height of 106 feet at $t = 2.5$,

What was its height at $t = 1$?

Solution:

There are variables in the equation, so the first job is to substitute values into the equation to solve for the constant.

Plugging in $t = 0$ at 6 feet:

$6 = c - (d - 4(0))^2$ which equals $6 = c - d^2$ or

$c = 6 + d^2$

Plug in $t = 2.5$ at 106 feet:

$106 = c - (d - 4(2.5))^2$

$106 = c - (d - 10)^2$

$106 = c - (d^2 - 20d + 100)$

Distribute the negative:

$106 = c - d^2 + 20d - 100$

Now, plug in the value of c into the equation:

$c = 6 + d^2$

$106 = 6 + d^2 - d^2 + 20d - 100$

Simplify:

$106 = 6 + 20d - 100$

$106 = 20d - 94$

Add 94 to both sides:

$200 = 20d$

$d = 10$.

Now, you can quickly find the value of c:

$c = 6 + d^2$

$ = 6 + (10)^2$

$ = 106$.

You were asked for the value of $t = 1$:

75

H(1) = 106 − (10 − 4(1))²
  = 106 − (6)²
  = 106 − 36 = 70.

***

PERCENT

Example:

The cost of an item was increased by 10 % and then the new price was decreased by 25%. The final price is what percent of the initial price?

Solution:

Note no amounts are given.

Always choose $100 because it is easy to work with!

Assume the cost of the item is $100.

It is increased by 10%, so now it is $110.

The new price is $110 and it is decreased by 25%.

.25 x $110 = $27.50.

So the new price is now, $110 – $27.50 = $82.50.

The final price = $82.50.

The question asks:

The final price is what percent of the initial price?

Simply, plug in the numbers:

82.50 equals what percent (x/100) of 100?

$$82.50 = \frac{x}{100} (100)$$

The 100 cancels on the right and you're left with:

82.50 %

Of course, you would not have needed to calculate the percent because you know that $82.50 is 82.50% of 100.

***

Remember:

Whenever you are calculating percent for a test grade you must multiply the answer by 100.

For example, if you received a 23/25 on a test, by dividing, you get .92. Multiplying that by 100 gives you your percentage: 92%.

***

Example:

There are 75 more women than men enrolled in Linden College. If there are n men enrolled, then in terms of n, what percent of those enrolled are men?

Solution:

# of women enrolled = n + 75

Total # enrolled = n + n + 75

or 2n + 75

Percentage of men enrolled =

$$\frac{n}{2n + 75}$$

Of course, that is one of the answer choices!

But, it is wrong, you must multiply the answer by 100 to get the percentage amount!

The correct answer is

$$\frac{n}{2n + 75} \times 100$$

***

Mean/Median/Mode:

When calculating the average or mean, most students know:

$$\frac{\text{Sum of the terms}}{\text{\# of terms}} = \text{average}$$

So, you could calculate the sum of the terms by multiplying the average by the # of terms:

Sum of the terms = average times (# of terms)

Example:

The average of 14 books is p pounds. In terms of p, what is the total weight of the books in pounds?

Answer: 14p

Example:

If the average of x + y = 5, and the average of x + y + z = 8, what is the value of z?

Solution:

We don't need to know the value of x or y to solve this problem.

Knowing the average of x + y = 5 means that the sum of x + y = 10.

Substituting x + y = 10 into x + y + z = 8,

$$\frac{10 + z}{3} = 8$$

10 + z = 24

z = 14.

***

Weighted Average Questions:

Example:

If 3 people got a 95 and 2 people got an 85, what is the average?

Make sure you don't quickly add 95 and 85 and divide by 2 to get 90!

$$\frac{3(95) + 2(85)}{5} = \frac{285 + 170}{5} = \frac{455}{5} = 91$$

***

Probability:

If you are told the probability of an event but not the total number of possibilities, the total number of possibilities must be divisible by the denominator.

Example:

If the probability of picking an apple from a bag of fruit is 2:5, could 52 be the total number of pieces of fruit in the bag?

No – because 52 is not divisible by 5.

If the probability of picking an apple is 2:5, then that means for every 5 pieces of fruit, two of them are apples.

***

You should know the Fundamental Counting Principle and how to solve permutations:

Fundamental Counting Principal:

If one selection can be made "m" ways and the 2nd selection can be made "n" ways, the # of ways 2 selections can be made is m x n.

***

# of permutations of n objects arranged in a <u>definite order</u> = n!

***

# of ways you can choose or arrange items when <u>not</u> all of them are used:

So, if you need to choose r items from a group of n where <u>order matters</u>:

$$_nP_r = \frac{n!}{(n-r)!}$$

***

Example: If you have 5 books, how many ways can you arrange 3 of them? Here, order matters. Arranging the books 123 is different than arranging the same books 321.

Answer: $$_5P_3 = \frac{5!}{(5-3)!} = \frac{5 \times 4 \times 3 \times 2 \times 1}{2 \times 1} = \frac{120}{2}$$

$$= 60.$$

***

If you need to choose r items from a group of n where <u>order doesn't matter</u>:

$$_nC_r = \frac{n!}{r!(n-r)!}$$

Example: (Exact question was on an SAT exam – one of the last, most difficult problems)

If you had 4 types of meat and 5 types of vegetables, how many ways can you choose 1 meat and 2 vegetables?

Solution:

1. Calculate how many ways you can choose 1 meat out of 4 choices. Obviously, you can choose 1 meat 4 different ways.

2. Calculate how many ways you can choose 2 vegetables from 5 vegetables:

Order doesn't matter here so we'll use:

$$_nC_r = \frac{n!}{r!(n-r)!}$$

$$_5C_2 = \frac{5!}{2!(5-2)!} = \frac{5 \times 4 \times 3 \times 2 \times 1}{2(3 \times 2 \times 1)} =$$

$$120/12 = 10.$$

4 different meats paired with a possible 10 selections of 2 vegetables = 40.

***

Example:

If you have 5 different cards, how many ways can they be arranged if one of them can never be in the first or fifth position?

Solution:

Without the condition of the first or fifth position, it is a straightforward permutation:

Remember: # of permutations of n objects arranged in a <u>definite order</u> = n!

5 x 4 x 3 x 2 x 1 = 120 ways you can arrange 5 different cards.

Now – students must subtract the number of times that one book could be in the first position. They would have 4 choices for the 2nd position, 3 for the third, etc… or 4 x 3 x 2 x 1 = 24.

The number of times a book could be in the 5th position, which is the same, 24.

The answer is 120 – 24 – 24 = 72.

***

Memorize:

These equations are not given on the exam.

$Y = kx$ is for <u>direct proportion.</u>

$xy = k$ for <u>indirect proportion.</u>

***

<u>**Exponents:**</u>

Add exponents when you <u>multiply</u> like bases.

(not add like bases)

Multiply exponents when you raise a power to a power.

Note: DO NOT ADD EXPONENTS WHEN <u>ADDING</u> LIKE BASES!

EXAMPLE:

$2^x + 2^x + 2^x + 2^x = 128$ Solve for x.

Solution:

$4(2^x) = 128$

$2^x = 128/4 = 32.$

$2^x = 32 \quad x = 5$

***

Remember:

When you multiply two numbers in Scientific Notation, multiply the numbers and then you add the exponents.

Example:

$(7 \times 10^2)(4 \times 10^5) = 28 \times 10^7 = 2.8 \times 10^8$

When <u>adding</u> numbers in Scientific notations do not add the numbers and then the exponents!

$(2 \times 10^4) + (5 \times 10^3) + (6 \times 10^2) + (4 \times 10^1) =$

$20,000 + 5000 + 600 = 40 = 25,640.$

***

Example:

$(6 \times 10^{-8}) + (1 \times 10^{-8}) = 7 \times 10^{-8}$

Because they both have the same exponent, you can add the numbers.

***

Here's an example of a problem where you solve for variables in terms of other variables with rational exponents:

(This problem would definitely be the last problem on an SAT exam and considered most difficult.)

Example:

$X^{-4/3} = K^{-2}$ and $y^{4/3} = n^2$

What is $(xy)^{-2/3}$ in terms of n and k?

Solution:

Step 1: Distribute the -2/3 power to both the x and the y in $(xy)^{-2/3}$:

$x^{-2/3} y^{-2/3}$

Step 2: We know the value of K^{-2} and n^2, we need to isolate k and n (solve for k and solve for n).

So,

Given $x^{-4/3} = k^{-2}$, rewrite:

$$= \frac{1}{(\sqrt[3]{x})^4} = \frac{1}{k^2} \quad \text{or} \quad (\sqrt[3]{x})^4 = k^2$$

$(\sqrt[3]{x})^4 = k^2$ simplifies into $(\sqrt[3]{x})^2 = k$ or

$x^{-2/3} = k^{-1}$

$y^{4/3} = n^2$

$(\sqrt[3]{y})^4 = n^2$ or $(\sqrt[3]{y})^2 = n$

$y^{-2/3} = n^{-1}$

Now that you know the value of

$x^{-2/3} y^{-2/3}$, you can substitute:

Remember the question asks:

What is $(xy)^{-2/3}$ in terms of n and k?

$x^{-2/3} y^{-2/3}$ in terms of n and k = $(k^{-1})(n^{-1})$ or $1/kn$

Review what you did to solve this problem:

Distributed an exponent to each variable

Re-wrote a negative exponent as 1/value

Took the square root of an exponent

***

Students should know the doubling time growth formula:

$N = N_0 \times 2^{t/d}$

***

Students should know the Exponential Growth Formula:

$Y = a \times b^x$ where x = # of years,

b = growth factor, a = the starting amount.

Example:

The cost of maintenance on an auto increases each year by 10%. Andrew paid $300 this year for maintenance. If the cost, c, for maintenance on the auto n years from now is

$C(n) = 300 \, x^n$, what is the value for x?

Solution:

Know: For exponential growth, add 100% to the percent increase:

Percent increase + 100 % in decimal form.

The increase for this problem was 10%.

Adding 100% to 10% gives you 110% or 1.1.

Answer is 1.1.

When you know the formula, $Y = a \times b^x$, and how to calculate the growth factor, you get the answer very quickly.

***

Be familiar with rewriting the base of exponents.

Example:

$2^{2x} = 8^{x-1}$ Solve for x.

Solution:

Rewrite the base so they are equal: $2^3 = 8$

$2^{2x} = 2^{3(x-1)}$

Now you can set the exponents equal to solve for x:

$2x = 3(x - 1)$

$2x = 3x - 3$

$3 = x$

Example:

$4(2^x) = 2^y$ Solve for x in terms of y.

Solution:

Rewrite 4 as 2^2

$2^2(2^x) = 2^y$

$2^{2+x} = 2^y$

(when you multiply like bases, add the exponents)

Now the bases are the same and you can set the exponents equal to each other and solve.

$2 + x = y$ or $x = y - 2$.

***

GEOMETRY:

Remember:

The triangle with the longest base will have the longest hypotenuse.

***

The measure of the angle between the hypotenuse and the base will be the smallest for the triangle with the longest hypotenuse.

***

If you know the slope of the hypotenuse of a right triangle and the legs are parallel to the x-axis and y-axis, the slope will equal the length of leg y (change in y) divided by the length of leg x (the change in the x).

***

A line perpendicular (an horizontal line) to the y-axis will have the equation y = a constant number.

A line perpendicular (a vertical line) to the x-axis will have the equation x = a constant number.

***

Given a picture of a line on a graph showing the y-intercept and one other point, you can calculate the slope.

***

Understand that if you have a line with a slope = -1/3 and you multiply the slope by -3, you'll get a new slope of 1, which will have a graph increasing from left to right but will still have the same y-intercept.

***

Another example of multiplying the slope:

If you have a graph with a positive slope of 1 and you multiply that slope by 2, you'll have a graph with a sharper angle going up from left to right with the same y-intercept.

***

Right Triangles:

You can have a right triangle with sides 3, 4, 5 and 5, 12, 13. So, if you're given a triangle with sides 9 and 12, you can notice that they are multiples of 3, and 4 so the last side must be a multiple of 5 = 15.

Just as 6, 8, 10 is a multiple of 3, 4, 5.

***

Memorize:

Triangle Inequality Theorem:

The sum of any two sides of a triangle must be > than the third side.

***

If 2 chords have the same length, then they are the same distance from the center of the circle.

***

Vertical Angles are congruent.

***

All angles around a point = 360 degrees.

***

The **sum of the interior angles** of a polygon can be found by drawing all diagonals of the polygon from one vertex and multiplying the number of triangles formed by 180 degrees.

***

Perimeter of a rectangle = 2L + 2W

A cube has all equal sides and 6 faces.

Surface area of a cube = $6s^2$.

***

Volume = the amount of space an object takes up.

***

Diagonals of rectangle are congruent.

Area of a sector = (area of circle)(sector %)

Arc length = (degrees)(Π/180)r

Sector % = degrees of angle divided by 360

Sector percentage tells you the fraction of the area of the sector to the total area of the circle.

If you're asked what fraction is the area of a sector to the total area of the circle, all you need is the degrees of the angle of the sector. Divide the degrees of the angle of the sector by 360.

(You don't need to know area of the sector or the area of circle)

***

Exterior angles of a polygon = 360.

Exterior angle of a triangle = sum of 2 non-adjacent interior angles.

Area of a trapezoid = ½ (b_1 + b_2)h

Circumference of a circle means length or distance around.

Negative slope = line decreasing from left to right

Positive slope = line increasing from left to right

***

Example:

One leg of a right triangle = 7 − x and the other

leg = 7 + x, and

the hypotenuse = 10,

what's $49 + x^2$?

Solution:

We know a right triangle satisfies $C^2 = a^2 + b^2$ where c = the hypotenuse and a and b represent each leg of the right triangle.

$10^2 = (7 - x)^2 + (7 + x)^2$

$100 = 49 - 14x + x^2 + 49 + 14x + x^2$

$100 = 49 + x^2 + 49 + x^2$

$100 = 2(49 + x^2)$ (divide both sides by 2)

$50 = 49 + x^2$

***

ABSOLUTE VALUE:

Students should practice translating a word problem into an absolute value inequality sentence.

Given: the difference in the actual number, n, and the ideal number 12, must be less than or equal to 1/8.

This translates to

$|n - 12| \leq 1/8.$

MUST MEMORIZE:

$|A| \leq b$ **means you solve** $-b \leq A \leq b$
Another way to write $-b \leq A \leq b$ would be
$A \leq b$ **AND** $A \geq -b$

$|A| \geq b$ **means you solve** $A \leq -b$ **OR** $A \geq b$

So, it doesn't matter whether the absolute value problem involves less than or greater than, you solve the same 2 problems. The only difference is one is OR and one is AND.

An easy association is: the "greater than" word has an "r" in it, so that's the one with OR.

The "less than" word doesn't have an "r," so that's the one with AND.

***

Graphs:

Example:

You might be given a graph without the equation for the graph and be asked what is the value of h(5)?

Solution:

Look at 5 on the x-axis and find the y-value.

***

Example:

Given a graph of y = g(x) and told g(2) = k.

Solve g(k).

Solution:

Look at the x-axis for the value of 2 and see where the graph is for the y-value at that point.

That is the value of k.

Now, you can solve g(k).

***

Example:

y = 5x – 10 and the line crosses the x-axis at (a,b). What's the value of a?

Solution:

Where the graph crosses the x-axis, y = 0 and where the graph crosses the y-axis, x = 0.

So, what they're asking is when y = 0, what is the value of x.

0 = 5x – 10.

10 = 5x

x = 2

***

Memorize the graphs:

$y = x^2$,

$y = 3x^2$,

$y = -3x^2$,

$y = (½)x^2$.

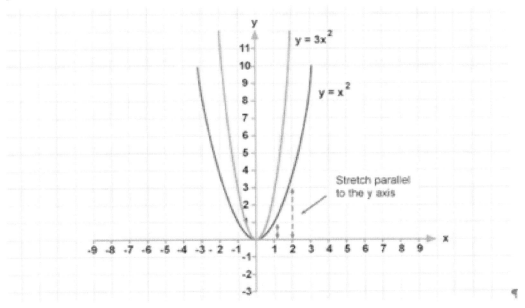

$Y = (½) x^2$ will be wider than the graph of $y = x^2$.

You can also graph the $y = -3x^2$ and realize that it will look exactly like $y = 3x^2$ but it will open downward.

***

Memorize:

Given a graph of y = x, written f(x) = x,

what is the graph of f(x + 2)?

Solution:

The graph will be shifted two units to the <u>left.</u>

***

Know the graph of f(x – 2) will be shifted 2 units to the right.

Know the graph of f(x+2) will be shifted 2 units to the left.

Know the graph of f(x) + 2 will be shifted 2 units up.

Know the graph of f(x) – 2 will be shifted 2 units down.

The graph of f(x + 2) + 2 will be shifted 2 units to the left and 2 units up.

***

Know the graph: $y = ax^2 + bx + c$.

When a > 0, when a is positive, the graph opens upward.

When a < 0, when a is negative, the graph opens downward.

When c > 0, it will cross the y-axis above the x-axis.

When c < 0, it will cross the y-axis below the x-axis.

The solution of a quadratic equation, $y = ax^2 + bx + c$, are the values of x when y = 0. So, given an equation in the form $y = ax^2 + bx + c$, you would set y = 0 and solve: $0 = ax^2 + bx + c$.

***

Percent Problems:

Percent Increase = increase/original

Percent Decrease = decrease/original.

***

Average Speed:

Be able to calculate the average speed:

Average Speed = total distance/total time.

Know: If someone travels at 2 different speeds for 2 different lengths of time, the average speed is NOT the average of the 2 speeds. It is similar to a weighted average.

***

Know:

Distance = rate x time

To solve distance word problems:

For same direction travel: set the two equations equal.

For round trip travel: set the 2 equations equal.

For opposite direction travel: add the 2, set them equal to total distance.

***

Sets:

Most students know that the union of 2 sets means all the elements in both sets.

Recognize, the union, the common elements, means you must subtract the common elements from the union of 2 sets twice because they are in both sets!

***

More Algebra:

Zero is neither positive nor negative!!

***

Translate minutes into seconds for m minutes:

$$\frac{m \text{ minutes} \times 60 \text{ seconds}}{1 \text{ minute}} = 60m \text{ seconds}$$

***

Given the dimensions of a room in feet, know how many square yards:

<u>1 square yard = 9 square feet</u>

A room is 10 feet by 15 feet = 150 square feet

How many square yards is a 10 feet by 15 feet?

$$150 \text{ square feet} \times \frac{1 \text{ square yard}}{9 \text{ square ft}} = 16.6666 \text{ square yards.}$$

To convert square feet into square yards, you divide by 9.

***

Know Greatest Common Factor versus Least Common Denominator: GCF and LCM.

Here's a trick to remember:

Given 2 numbers and asked for both the GCF and the LCM:

Factor both numbers:

For the GCF, you will take only the common factors and for the

LCM, you will take the common factors and the other factors.

You can remember this by:

For GCF – factors are few (only take the common factors)

For LCM – multiples are many (take the common factors and the others)

***

Example:

What is the GCF and LCM for 20 and 15?

Solution:

Factor each number:

20 = 10 x 2 or 2 x 5 x 2

15 = 5 x 3

For the GCF only take the common factors: 5

For the LCM take common and others: 5 x 2 x 2 x 3 = 60.

***

Know: If a number is a factor of 2 different numbers, then it is also a factor of one of those numbers minus the other:

In the above example: 5 is a factor of 15 and 20. It is also a factor of 20 – 15 = 5.

***

Example:

If n and p are integers greater than 1 and if p is a factor of both n+ 3 and n+ 10, what is the value of p?

Knowing that if a number is a factor of 2 different numbers, then it is also a factor of one of those numbers minus the other:

Solution:

n + 10 – (n + 3)= p

n – 10 – n - 3 = p

7 = p

∗∗∗

Memorize the Prime Numbers to 30:
2, 3, 5, 7, 11, 13, 17, 19, 23, 29

***

Know the addition and multiplication of odd and even numbers:

Addition: even + even = even

even + odd = odd

odd + odd = even

Multiplication: even x even = even

even x odd = even

odd x odd = odd

***

Example:

If x, y and z are positive integers such that x + y is even, and the value of $(x + y)^2 + x + z$ is odd, which of the following must be true?

a) x is odd

b) x is even

c) if z is even, then x is odd

d) if z is even, then xy is even

e) xy is even

Solution:

If x + y is even, then either x and y are both even or x and y are both odd.

2 possibilities:

First possibility:

If they are even, then $(x + y)^2 = (x + y) \times (x + y)$ = even x even = even.

Then, $(x + y)^2 + x + z$ = even + even + z.

Knowing even + even = even then z must be odd for the whole thing to = odd.

Second possibility:

If x and y are both odd, then $(x + y)^2$ = even x even = even

Because (odd + odd = even)

$(x + y)^2 + x$ = even + odd = odd so z must be even

C is the answer that is true.

I think the fastest way to solve this might be to plug in values.

Knowing that the only way x + y = even is if they are both odd or both even.

Try 1, the value of x and the value of y are both even:

x = 2 y = 2

$(x + y)^2 + x + z$ is odd

4 x 4 = 16 + 2 = 18

18 + z = odd, so if x and y are both even, z must be odd.

Try 2, the value of x and the value of y are both odd:

x = 3, y = 3

3 + 3 = 6

6 x 6 = 36 + 3 = 39

39 + z is odd

so if x and y are odd, then z must be even = choice c.

***

Consecutive Integer Problems:

Example:

If the least integer = -25, and the sum of the consecutive integers = 26, how many integers are there in the set?

Solution:

- 25 + ……… + -1 + 0 + 1+ ……. + 25 = 0 + 26 = 26

So, how many integers between -25 and positive 26?

50 + the integer 0 plus the integer 26 = 52

Zero is one of the integers!

When you have negative numbers in a consecutive integer set, 0 is included.

***

Example:

If $x^2 + y^2 = 73$ and $xy = 24$, what is the value of

$(x + y)^2$?

Solution:

Multiply out $(x + y)^2$ to get $x^2 + 2xy + y^2$ and then you can easily substitute the values in to get

$73 + 24 = 121$.

You never know the individual values for x and y and you don't need to in order to solve this problem.

***

Example:

If $xy = 7$ and $x - y = 5$, then $x^2y - xy^2 = ?$

Solution:

Factor x and y out of $x^2y - xy^2$:

$xy(x - y) =$

$7(5) = 35$

This is another example of not knowing the individual values of x and y.

***

Arithmetic Sequences:

For all sequences that have a common difference, use the formula:

$A_n = A_1 + (n - 1)d$

Where n equals the value at the nth position in the sequence, d equals the difference and A_1 equals the first number in the sequence.

***

Example:

Find the 10th value in the sequence:

5, 8, 11, 14, 17

Solution:

The difference between each term is 3.

You add three to get the next term.

Using $A_n = A_1 + (n - 1)d$:

$5 = A_1$, $n = 10$, and $d = 3$:

Solve: $5 + (10 - 1)3$ to find the 10th value in the sequence.

$5 + 9(3) =$

$5 + 27$

32

***

Reflections:

Memorize:

A reflection in the x-axis means (x, y) → (x, -y)

Example:

Reflect Line L about the x-axis, the new line M has slope – 4/5.

What's the slope of the original line L?

Solution:

Slope = 4/5

***

Advice on the Essay for the SAT Exam

You have 25 minutes to write an essay on the front and back of a lined sheet of paper.

DO NOT WRITE OUTSIDE THE LINES. Your essay is scanned into a computer and will not pick up anything outside the lines on the sheet.

Make sure your writing is legible. If the reader cannot make out a word, it will take away from the strength of your essay.

You MUST write about the topic you are assigned. If you do not, you will receive a zero no matter how brilliantly you wrote.

You must agree or disagree with the statement. There is no right answer. They are looking for a convincing argument, not the correct answer.

To prepare for the writing section before you take the actual exam, make a list of all the historical facts you can remember in your history courses and all the classic novels you read listing the themes and a few examples for each theme from each book.

The highest scoring essays contain an example from a novel or history along with an example from your experiences or observations.

During the exam, decide on your opinion and jot down 3 examples that support your point of view in the first 5 minutes. Write for 15 minutes and in the last 5 minutes, read your essay.

Things you should be familiar with for writing the essay on the SAT exam:
EXAMPLES FROM HISTORY:

ROMAN HISTORY – CAESAR

FRENCH REVOLUTION

AMERICAN REVOLUTION

CIVIL RIGHTS 1950'S

SOUTH AFRICA

RUSSIAN REVOLUTION

TECNOLOGY

WHAT ARE THE COSTS OF TECHNOLOGIAL ADVANCEMENT – GOOD/BAD?

Internet – who created it?

Cotton Gin

Cars

Atomic Bomb

CHERNOBAL

Censorship – good or bad? The Cold War

Women's Rights

Iraq – force as a means to an end – good or bad?

Civil Rights Movement

Examples from all the literature you have read.

If you forgot the themes from any novel you read, read the summary of themes on sparknotes.com.

Definitely practice writing a couple of essays. At first, you don't have to time it just to get the feel of writing an essay in the allotted space. After you get the hang of it, write an essay in the 25 minutes. You can find all the practice essays in any SAT study guidebook.

***

Below are a student's notes on some historical facts, some of the novels she read and some general outlines of possible essays you should be familiar with.

***

Definitely practice an essay on technological advancement; it's a common question on SAT exams.

WHAT ARE THE COSTS OF TECHNOLOGIAL ADVANCEMENT – GOOD/BAD?

Here are notes to review on technology:

INTERNET   - know who created it:

INTERNET

The Internet is a worldwide network of thousands of computers and computer networks. It is a public, voluntary, and cooperative effort between the connected institutions and is not owned or operated by any single organization. The Internet and Transmission Control Protocols were initially developed in 1973 by American computer scientist Vinton Cerf as part of a project sponsored by the United States Department of Defense Advanced Research Projects Agency (ARPA) and directed by American engineer Robert Kahn.

The Internet began as a computer network of ARPA (ARPAnet) that linked computer

networks at several universities and research laboratories in the United States.

The World Wide Web was developed in 1989 by English computer scientist

Timothy Berners-Lee for the European Organization for Nuclear Research (CERN).

"The design of the Internet was done in 1973 and published in 1974. There ensued about

10 years of hard work, resulting in the roll out of Internet in 1983.

COTTON GIN

Eli Whitney (December 8, 1765 – January 8, 1825) was an American inventor best known as the inventor of the cotton gin. It made it much easier to remove the seeds from cotton. The machine was 5000 percent more efficient than a human being. This was one of the key inventions of the Industrial Revolution and shaped the economy of the antebellum South.[1] <u>Whitney's invention made short staple cotton into a profitable crop, which strengthened the economic foundation of slavery.</u>

Invented in 1793

It made it easier and cheaper to use cotton. Demand grew. Cotton production grew. Cotton farming is labor intensive so it intensified the South's dependence on slave labor.

Thomas Edison 1876 – invented the light bulb

His inventions allowed for the extension of the workday. These inventions generated greater opportunities for mass production, which then caused the <u>economy to grow</u> and the captains of industry who owned and controlled the new manufacturing enterprises became <u>extremely rich and powerful</u> during this period.

CARS

Two Germans, Carl Benz and Gottlieb Daimler, both took credit for making the first car. Eventually the car companies that they founded combined to become the Daimler-Benz Company, which still produces Mercedes-Benz automobiles more than 100 years later.

In 1908, Henry Ford started the Ford Motor Company, which became famous for building the Model T, which sold for $850 at first.

The mass use of motor vehicles was bound to have some unforeseen and undesirable consequences, of which three can be singled out: **traffic congestion, air pollution, and highway accidents.**

A historian has said that Henry Ford freed common people from the limitations of their geography. The automobile created mobility on a scale never known before, and **the total effect on living habits and social customs is endless.**

The automobile has radically changed city life by accelerating the outward expansion of population into the suburbs. The suburban trend is emphasized by the fact that highway transportation encourages business and industry to move outward to sites where land is cheaper, where access by car and truck is easier than in crowded cities, and where space is available for their one or two story structures

Before the automobile, people both lived in the city and worked in the city, or lived in the country and worked on a farm. Because of the automobile, the growth of suburbs has allowed people to live on the outskirts of the city and be able to work in the city by commuting. New jobs due to the impact of the automobile such as fast food, city/highway construction, state patrol/police, convenience stores, gas stations, auto repair shops, auto shops, etc. allow more employment for the world's growing population.

ATOM BOMB

In 1939, Physicist, Edward Teller was part of the group of scientists that <u>invented the atomic bomb</u> as part of the Manhattan Project. He was the co-founder of Lawrence Livermore National Laboratory, where <u>together with Ernest Lawrence, Luis Alvarez, and others he invented the hydrogen bomb in 1951.</u>

The 2005 report prepared by the Chernobyl Forum, led by the International Atomic Energy Agency (IAEA) and World Health Organization (WHO), attributed 56 direct deaths (47 accident workers, and nine children with thyroid cancer), and estimated that there may be 4,000 extra cancer deaths among the approximately 600,000 most highly exposed people.[1] Although the Chernobyl Exclusion Zone and certain limited areas remain off limits, the majority of affected areas are now considered safe for settlement and economic activity.

Broad Impacts of Nuclear Power Deployment

Primary Impact

   a)Economic

   direct cost savings

   Fossil fuel price capping

   Energy supply security (avoided lost output)

   Avoided net fuel imports

   Enhanced technology exports

   Electricity price stability

   Intellectual capital gains

   b)Environmental/Health Increased radiation

   Nuclear accident consequences

   Avoided greenhouse gas emissions

   Avoided acid gas emissions

   Avoided carcinogen emissions

   Avoided fuel extraction and transport accidents

   c)Social

   changed employment levels

   changed risk perceptions

   (weapons, accidents, health gene pool)

   changed social consensus

   changed cultural impact

   changed ecological impacts

Economic Consequences

    enhanced productivity

    improved competition

    improved terms of trade

    currency appreciation and enhanced economic growth

    changed levels of morbidity and mortality, therefore economic output

    changed physical damage and environmental losses affecting resource utilization

    direct effects on resources

    changed institutional costs

    changed economic efficiency

CHERNOBAL – example of the negative impact of nuclear technology

The Chernobyl disaster was a nuclear reactor accident that occurred on 26 April 1986 at the Chernobyl Nuclear Power Plant in Ukraine (then part of the Soviet Union). It is considered to be the worst nuclear power plant disaster in history and the only level 7 event on the International Nuclear Event Scale.

Two sample outlines for an essay on technology:

One saying technology is a good thing and one for technology being bad:

Technology/Good:

Internet:

Connects millions of people, relatives across the world

News spreads faster

Protestant Reformation

Information more accessible

Medicine, healing, new scientific discoveries

Printing Press

Johannes Gutenburg's invention of moveable type changed the intellectual world forever. It allowed classical learning to spread, the Reformation to reach the masses, popular literature to develop, and prevented scientific discoveries from languishing unread. Spreading ideas faster, the printing press encouraged the development of scholarly research and the desire to attain knowledge. It facilitated cooperation among scholars and helped produce standardized texts. It also stimulated the development of an educated, literate public, in contrast to the medieval society in which only three to four percent of the population could read.

Light Bulb:

Thomas Edison's invention allowed for the extension of the workday, as people became able to work into the night. The light bulb generated greater opportunities for mass production, which then caused the economy to grow and the captains of industry who owned and controlled the new manufacturing enterprises became extremely rich and powerful during this period. The lower classes also benefitted, as it allowed them to work extra hours and therefore earn extra wages. It also opened up more jobs, including the assembly line of mass-producing light bulbs.

Technology/Bad:

Internet:

False info

No rules to assure accuracy, content – Wikipedia

Identity theft

News spreads faster: Osama Bin Laden and Al Queda can spread their message to a wider audience

Cotton gin:

Although many assume Eli Whitney's invention to be a great thing for society since it exponentially skyrocketed production of cotton in the American South, the cotton gin also ruined thousands of lives. By increasing cotton production and profits, the cotton gin also increased southern dependence on cotton, and therefore slavery. In addition, as more and more slaves were needed and exploited, tensions escalated between North and South.

Thus, the invention of the cotton gin may have increased profits for the greedy landowners, but it also indirectly led to the civil war.

Nuclear Energy:

In theory, nuclear energy is a great development for its use drastically would clean up the environment and reduce fossil fuel emissions. However, humans run nuclear plants, and humans make mistakes. Any slight mistake in the operation regulation, or maintenance of a single nuclear plant results in huge amounts radioactivity released into the environment. For example, there was a nuclear disaster at the Chernobyl plant in Ukraine in 1986. It resulted in a severe release of radioactivity following a massive power excursion that destroyed the reactor. While there were many deaths caused by the explosion, a vast amount of people died from the radiation that followed. Thousands developed cancer. Some parts of the area are still off-limits even today. Also, nuclear fuel remains toxic for centuries after its use, and no effective and safe storage area has been designed. For these reasons, the benefits of the development of nuclear energy are outweighed by the risks it poses.

***

Another essay topic you should be familiar with is censorship.

CENSORSHIP: Bad

Cold War

Berlin Wall: East Berlin under USSR rule, ideas of democracy were banned. The censorship made ideas of democracy like a forbidden fruit, as the people yearned for unbiased news instead of the Soviet's propaganda. The US occupational authorities created RIAS, a radio station to provide the German population in and around Berlin – both American and Soviet sectors - with unbiased news and political reporting. It quickly had a huge audience in East Germany and was the most popular foreign radio service. The Soviet's censorship backfired, as they now appeared hypocritical in front of their people, who gravitated towards the unbiased news of the Americans, and eventually called for their own democracy.

CHURCH

Pope Pius IX: Syllabus of Errors: condemned every criticism of the Church as heresy. It condemned freedom of religion and separation of church and state, even though Jesus himself called for separation of Church and state. This was looked at as hypocrisy from the church. It was a list of "condemned positions" without explaining why each was wrong. The church could not combat the advance of science and critical analysis, so they just adopted narrow-minded opposition

Pope Leo XIII announced that the Bible, and the Church, "must be incapable of teaching error"

Pius X issued another index of forbidden books containing the following influential authors:

Descartes

Locke - Essay Concerning Human Understanding

Voltaire - Letters of the Philosophes

Diderot - The Encyclopedia

Rousseau - The Social Contract

Gibbon - Rise and Fall of the Roman Empire

Thomas Paine - The Rights of Man

Darwin - Origin of Species

Flaubert - Madame Bovary

Be familiar with the American Revolution, the French revolution, and the Chinese Revolution.

Conservatism vs. Revolutionary-ism – Revolution-ism was always stronger

American

French

Chinese

***

Women's rights – 3 examples of women's negative impact on society not having equal rights:

Women in 19th century: 2nd class citizens:

Education:

Couldn't get education past elementary school, only taught domestic skills

Excluded from medical school

Women's colleges not taken seriously

Jobs

Could only get menial jobs

Lack of education

Slop work + sweat shops – piecework, poverty,

Little wages

Society

Prostitution – tolerated and regulated

Couldn't own property or vote or divorce

Men dominated legal system, Contagious Disease Act persecuted women, not men

Women in Totalitarian Regimes

Nazi Germany: backseat

Hitler wanted to separate sexes

Banned women in political life

Incentives to have large family

Mussolini's Italy: backseat

Domestic roles forced

Propaganda, laws

Tax breaks for bigger family

Mussolini tried to remove them from work force

Stalinist Russia: backseat

Special women sector in Party was abolished

Social/sexual relationships inferior to political and economic ones

Feminist Movement:

    Started in US by Elizabeth Stanton.

Britain = Suffragettes

    Contemporary phase: 1960's in US, sparked by civil rights movement

***

Invasion of Iraq: force means to an end?

Yes: Hussein had been warned numerous times to disarm by the UN but had refused, and he had attacked his own people with chemical weapons

No: No WMD's found, Iraq not directly responsible for 9.11, questionable goals (oil?)

Civil Rights Movement:

Montgomery Bus Boycott: 1955-1956

- Blacks boycott of Montgomery's bus system
- Resulted in crippling of finances for city's public transportation system
- Started when Rosa Parks refused to surrender her seat to a white person, and ended when the Supreme Court declared the Alabama and Montgomery laws requiring segregated buses unconstitutional.

Greensboro Sit-ins

- Students of a nearby black college sat down at the whites-only section of a restaurant. The first day 4 students participated, by the 4th day 300 students were there
- Their demonstrations sparked similar sit-ins all over N. Carolina
- Sometimes violent, but received significant gov + media attention

Selma to Montgomery Marches – peak of civil rights movement

- **Amelia Boynton** brought together many civil rights leaders for her voting rights movement
- **Bloody Sunday:** 600 civil rights marchers were attacked by state/local police with clubs and tear gas
- Marched 50+ miles from Selma to Montgomery
- Origin: blacks in Dallas County, Alabama, tried to go all together to register to vote, but were blocked by police + KKK. The blacks in Alabama struggled for vote but were denied, arrested, and killed.
- Media showed the attacks, Bloody Sunday, and civil rights gained more and more support. The marches drastically shifted public opinion about Civil rights movement as a whole. The images of Alabama law enforcement beating the nonviolent protesters were shown all over the country and the world by the television networks and newspapers. The visuals of such brutality being carried out by the state of Alabama helped shift the image of the segregationist movement from one of a movement trying to preserve the social order of the South to a system of state endorsed terrorism against those non-whites.
- **Resulted in Voting Rights Act of 1965**

***

Fredrick Douglass
- Born a slave
- As he got older he learned to read by observing he white children in the neighborhood and the writings of the men he worked with
- Learned about freedom and opened his mind to question slavery
- Eventually escaped slavery by sneaking aboard a train and faking his papers, and ended up in NY
- He joined a church and became a member of several anti-slavery societies
- He wrote his autobiography, the Narrative of the Life of Fredrick Douglass, an American Slave, and it quickly became a best seller.
- He traveled the United Kingdom to escape the possibility of his master recalling him, and acquired fame. British supporters purchased his freedom.

He returned to US and produces several abolitionist newspapers, and became a face of the abolitionist movement.

EXAMPLES FROM LITERATURE:

Here are a few examples from one student who took notes on a few of the novels she read before the SAT.

Read her notes and go back and make a list of the books you have read, their themes and a few examples from those themes so you can easily remember them during the essay.

***

1. 1984

Totalitarianism: government controls every aspect of life, even thought

Censorship: the Party controls the past, allowing them free reign in the present

Technology: the Party controls all aspects of life with technology- hidden microphones and cameras; computers and instruments of Orwell's imagination are used for torture, war, and enabling the actions of the party.

2. HUCK FINN

Racism and Slavery: Twain tells the story of the journey of a slave, Jim, through the eyes of a white, innocent young boy (Huck) and is not afraid to use "nigger" or expose the cruelty of slavery.

Hypocrisy of "civilized" society: Twain depicts society as a collection of degrading rules and precepts that defy logic. Jim, the slave, is the only one able to provide Huck with a father figure, and displays greater character than any of the white people in the novel.

Education: Huck disregards the morals that his flawed society has tried to teach him: prejudice. Huck, in fact, chooses to go to hell rather than follow the rules he has been taught. Twain's biggest complaint with society is the way it teaches its flawed morals to its youth.

3. GREAT EXPECTTIONS

Self-improvement/Social Class: by the end of the novel Pip learns that moral worth is more important than social class. He sees that Drummle, an upper class lout, has less integrity than Magwitch, an escaped convict

Possibility of reformation: Dickens questions the justice system as Magwitch, one of the novel's best characters, is thrown away for years because of his debt

4. ANIMAL FARM

- Characters

o Napoleon: pig (Stalin) who emerges as leader after the rebellion, using military force to intimidate and manipulate

o Snowball: pig (Trotsky) who challenges Napoleon for power

o Boxer: cart-horse whose incredible strength helps the prosperity of the farm and the building of the windmill. He is too dim to actually think independently about the ideals of the farm and about the actions of the pigs. One of his mottos is Napoleon is always right. He is eventually sold by the pigs to a glue factory for whiskey money.

Themes:

o Not questioning authority:

The animals, representing the working class, display fatal naiveté in believing everything that the pigs tell them. The pigs, led by Napoleon, perpetually oppress the other animals for their own good, but none of the animals oppose them because they believe the propaganda being told to them. Boxer, for instance, fails to consider the ideals and actions of the pigs in their ruling of the farm, and in fact, one of his mottos is "Napoleon is always right." As a result of his naiveté, he is manipulated by the pigs, who eventually sell him for whiskey money.

5. ROMEO AND JULIET

Themes:

Love is so powerful it supersedes all other values, emotions and loyalties. Their love was more important than their families, or any other loyalties they had.

Love leads to the death of both characters. Their love was so powerful they were willing to commit suicide in order to preserve it.

Fate and the idea that Romeo and Juliet are destined for their fate of death and they constantly see omens leading to that conclusion.

6. TALE OF TWO CITIES

The value of one's life is based on the effect it had on others. At the beginning of the novel, Carton frequently lamented his life and declared himself "an enormous waste of life." But at the end of the novel, he sacrifices himself so that his loved ones, Lucie and Darnay, may escape, and he dies at peace, feeling that his life finally has meaning and worth. Carton assumes a Christ-like role as he becomes a selfless martyr whose death enables the happiness of his beloved and ensures his own immortality. His death secures a new peaceful life for Lucie, Darnay, and even himself, for his life gains value as he saves the lives of others. After his death, Dickens implies that like Christ, Carton will be resurrected, as he is reborn in the hearts of those he has died to save. Darnay and Lucie even name their child in his namesake. Similarly, the text implies that the death of the old regime in France prepares the way for the beautiful and renewed Paris that Carton envisions from the guillotine. Although Carton spends most of the novel in a life of apathy, the supreme selflessness of his final act speaks to a human capacity for change.

Inherit the Wind:

Characters:
- Cates = teacher
- Drummond – lawyer defends Cates
- Brady – prosecuting lawyer

Theme – not following the mob

- It took place in a small Southern society that also acted as a manipulated mob. Its members simply rejected Darwin's theory without even reading Darwin's book, simply because they were taught by the Church to reject it. They did not stop to think for themselves, they were a manipulated mob who surrendered the right to think

- Society is not left to; decide for themselves whether or not believe Darwin, instead they are taught to reject him by those in power who stand to lose if people started questioning society and its values.

400 Vocabulary Words for the SSAT

The top 400 vocabulary words every middle school student should know.

These are the top 400 vocabulary words that one of the best private middle schools hands out to their 7th graders to review over the summer before 8th grade.

Go to www.quizlet.com and create a free account.

Search for harvardmomadvice and you will find that group.

Click on the group and request to join the group.

After you have access to the group, you will find 9 sets of vocabulary words. The first 8 sets contain 50 words each.

Students can practice learning 50 words at a time.

The 9th group, called more SSAT words, is words that some of my students told me they had trouble with on the exam and were not in the first 400-word list.

Once you click on the first group of words to practice, I suggest you have your student **first click on the arrow to the right of the flash card to just go through all 50 words reading them and their definition to see if any are already familiar.**

After reading through the words, **have the student click on Learn and just hit enter as if you didn't know the correct vocabulary word for the definition displayed. Quizlet.com will have you type in the word so you can start to memorize the word and the meaning.**

After practicing learning the words many times, students can click on test and on the right hand side, type in the number 50 to be tested on all 50 and the type of tests you'd like to take. I think matching and multiple-choice test are great for memory.

You can have your student practice these 50 words at a time for 20 minutes a day, several times a week and I think you'll be surprised how many vocabulary words they can learn in a short amount of time.

If you have any questions that were not answered in this book, please visit our website at www.harvardmomadvice.com where you can anonymously ask any question and read our blog!